By
What
Authority

By What Authority

A Conversation on Teaching Among United Methodists

Editors
Elizabeth Box Price
Charles R. Foster

A Project of the United Methodist
Association of Professors of Christian
Education

Abingdon Press
Nashville

By What Authority

Copyright © 1991 by Abingdon Press

This book is printed on recycled, acid-free paper.

By what authority : a conversation on teaching among United Methodists / Charles R. Foster, Elizabeth Box Price, editors.

    p.   cm.

"A project of the United Methodist Association of Professors of Christian Education."

    ISBN 0-687-04556-8 (alk. paper)

    1. United Methodist Church (U.S.)—Teaching office. 2. Methodist Church—Education—United States. 3. Christian education—Philosophy. 4. United Methodist Church (U.S.)—Doctrines. 5. Methodist Church—United States—Doctrines. I. Foster, Charles R., 1937-   . II. Price, Elizabeth Box. III. United Methodist Association of Professors of Christian Education.

BX8377.B92   1991

268'.876—dc20   91-7714
                                                             CIP

MANUFACTURED IN THE UNITED STATES OF AMERICA

Contents

I.
INTRODUCTION

"What should the church teach?"; "Who should teach?"; and "How should the church teach?" are questions focused upon by church leaders from the apostles to the present in their concern for the continuity and renewal of the church. These questions have typically been identified with the teaching office of the church through the ages. They preoccupy the attention of church leaders at those times when the distinctive message of the gospel is in danger of dilution or distortion. Among United Methodists that concern can be heard today from Sunday school to seminary classrooms and from annual conference to national church agencies. That concern led the United Methodist Association of Professors of Christian Education to explore what does function authoritatively for United Methodist teaching. This book presents this group's conversation with the intent of expanding the discussion across the church.

In the essay that follows Elizabeth Price identifies some of the contemporary forces that make it important for leaders at all levels of the life of the church to focus their attention on the church's teaching. We invite you to enter this conversation by asking yourself what should be central to teaching among the people called United Methodists?

Elizabeth Box Price
Charles R. Foster

Chapter 1

Perspectives on Teaching Authority:
A Conversation for United Methodists

Elizabeth Box Price

United Methodists recently celebrated "two hundred years of grace and freedom." Rallying across the decades around the words of John Wesley, "As to all opinions which do not strike at the root of Christianity, we think and let think," they have used as guidelines scripture, tradition, reason, and experience to make decisions about matters of faith and discipleship. During the last two decades increasing diversity and complexity have marked United Methodist theological perspectives, educational assumptions, and cultural and ethical values. The educational leadership of the church has attempted to respond to and accommodate the challenges to be found in the diversification of church member expectations. Responses to these challenges may be seen in curriculum resources and educational policies that sought to incorporate and embrace the diverse appeals present in the church. But this attempt to be responsive to the diversity of United Methodist membership has also provoked a growing interest among many church leaders to identify distinctive United Methodist approaches to educational ministry.

In the midst of many issues pressing the church from evangelism, social outreach, and mission, some have begun to ask the church to examine an issue that affects and holds a pivotal influence over all other issues. Their concern centers on the need in the church for clarity on what comprises the core of the Christian faith. To be stated another way, the concern raises the question of whether there is anything authoritative in the church's teaching or distinctive to the Christian faith of United Methodists. These issues are all subsumed under the pressing concern of how United Methodism can maintain its apostolic task to present the gospel authentically for the sake of the world as well as for its own life.

The richness of diversity with its new and multiple perspectives has been received by some as an opportunity for growth, offering the possibility of inclusiveness and comprehensive vision. For others this diversity creates relativity, ambiguity, and paradox, causing an uneasiness that borders on panic. In response, the cry for limits, identity, conventions, and authority intensifies and accelerates. The mood shifts from one characterized by exploration and dialogue to one characterized by the establishment of boundaries and the securing of identity. The focal question is no longer "What different forms or approaches to faith are called for?" but, rather, "Is there a core to Christian faith? If so, what is that core?"

The worry over a lack of a distinctive United Methodist approach to the church's educational ministry has led some to identify the question of authority in teaching as a crucial issue for the denomination today. Several factors contribute to the concern in the church over the authority of its teaching. Some of these will be identified and discussed briefly.

1. The presence of pluralism, both cultural and theological, definitely challenges traditional views and expectations of what is authoritative. The church is set in the midst of a society of many cultures, many races, many languages, and many religions. The idea of a benign melting pot has been replaced by one of pluralism in which different entities maintain their

identities while blending into a whole. There is no longer a monolithic Protestant culture or a common shared life-style in the nation. Allen Moore points to the results: "Present history has placed the church in an open culture that is marked by great diversity, including a wide variety of religious expressions, belief systems, and moral assumptions. In fact, even within a given denomination a consensus on matters of faith and practice is difficult to achieve."[1]

The complexity of pluralism has created a response of passive indifference among some persons who are over-whelmed by increasing possibilities. It also "masks a genial confusion in which one tries to enjoy the pleasures of difference without ever committing oneself to any particular vision of resistance and hope."[2]

2. Richard Osmer identifies individualism and counter-modernizing forces to be phenomena that have had significant influence over the exercise of teaching authority. He points out that individualism designates the individual as the arbiter of life's meaning and purpose, which undercuts the authority of corporate and conciliar entities such as the church. On the other end of the spectrum, countermodernizing forces advocate the exclusive authority of one true faith: an authoritarianism that demands blind submission to absolute religious authority. Each of these phenomena creates a major mind-set for the culture that affects how authority is to be viewed and how it is to be related to the teaching ministry of the church.

3. The trend and spirit within ecumenical circles to recover the more classical traditions of Christian thought highlights the value of teaching authority. There has been renewed interest to define and describe the apostolic faith for the twentieth century. The Faith and Order Commission of the World Council of Churches is now using the Nicene-Constantinopolitan Creed as a test of the faith expression of Christian bodies. There has been a resurgence in seeking theological norms from the early

church. Especially in North America these trends have been reinforced by the resurgence of evangelical piety.[3] Out of this same mood, within United Methodism there has been a strong recovery of interest in Wesley. Across the church there is evidence of a more normative approach to doctrine and a renewal of interest in history for the answers to faith. The reclaiming of earlier traditions calls forth a certain character of and focus for teaching in the church.

4. At first glance, the United Methodist interest in teaching authority has tended to focus on symptoms such as declining Sunday school attendance. Bishop Richard Wilke describes in his book *And Are We Yet Alive?* a church in deep crisis. His concern centers on declining church school membership, a decrease in the number of teachers, and the lack of Bible study.[4] But these problems only point to issues more deeply rooted in a loss of identity and integrity and a loss of clarity of purpose and mission in the denomination. In the month preceding the 1988 General Conference, delegates engaged in a major debate over a proposed new doctrinal statement. Although this debate occurred in the context of theological diversity, anxiety about that diversity contributed to the sense of urgency of many participants in the need for the church to define itself. Politically active groups made their theological convictions known in committees charged with making reports to the General Conference as well as in the public sphere through articles in journals and newspapers. The debate culminated in a new doctrinal statement, which was finally approved by the 1988 General Conference. It also reflects a shift in the denomination's approach to theological reflection.

Mary Elizabeth Mullins Moore, in a following chapter, identifies several characteristics of this shift that will affect the church's approach to its teaching. She describes a more normative approach to doctrine. This shift is evident in the designation of Scripture as the primary *criterion* rather than source and *guideline* for doctrine. Two consequences for understanding the authority of teaching are important to identify. This shift toward Scripture as the norm leaves tradition, experience, and reason as more subservient sources for the church's teaching. It also emphasizes evangelism and incorporation into the church as the primary goals of teaching while limiting the function of critical reflection and ecclesial reformation.

Although this insight may underscore the motivation for the ongoing conversation about teaching authority in the quest to reclaim and prevent losses in denominational identity and membership and to hold on to what is distinctively Methodist, the discussion is actually much more comprehensive. It also focuses on questions traditionally associated with the teaching office: what should be taught, who has authority to teach, and where teaching should occur.

This larger conversation occurs across the church at every level. It is evident in local church committee decisions about curriculum resources or denominational programs. The struggle over curriculum content and method often leads to questions regarding who will and who is able to teach. Pastors caught up both in a business model of administration and ministries committed to a lay-centered concept of leadership express frustration over what the ordination charge to "take authority" to teach really means.

Education staff members of the denomination engage in the discussion as they wrestle with the many expectations of various constituencies in the church and seek to formulate an organizing principle for their work in the light of these expectations. The Sections on Christian Education and Church School Publications of the General Board of Discipleship have recently approved a proposal for a new document identifying a vision for denominational Christian Education policy that will replace *Foundations for Teaching and Learning in The United*

Methodist Church, the present education statement. The Council of Bishops recently began an investigation into the nature and character of the teaching office and their own relationship to it. The bishops of the church conducted a consultation in 1986 on the teaching role of the pastor. This consultation had as its purpose encouraging, enhancing, and supporting the teaching role of ordained ministers. The discussion among the bishops in regard to teaching authority has sought a way to enable a common identity and purpose around which United Methodists might gather.

The conversation has also occurred among Christian education faculty in United Methodist colleges, graduate schools, and seminaries, who have responsibility to equip ordained, consecrated, and certified leadership of congregational education. Recently, a task force of United Methodist Association of Professors of Christian Education, a professional organization composed of membership of these faculties, out of sensitivity to cultural pluralism raised questions and concerns about the multiple forms of Christian education to be found in the church. They assumed there was a need for even greater diversity. The direction of conversation soon began to focus around the problems of teaching authority and the need for a distinctive core to denominational identity.

The conversation regarding teaching authority throughout the church is always sensitive to authoritarian and authoritative perspectives. This means that there are two directions that affect an interpretation of teaching authority. The authoritarian approach seeks absolutes, defining propositions to be passed on without question. It deduces truth and calls for submission to it. On the other hand, an authoritative approach derives authority from processes that seriously attend to and struggle with the heritage of the faith. It recognizes multiplicity of meaning and wrestles with the diversity of sources within the context of parameters set through the evolving conciliar structures. The next several paragraphs will explore the presence of these two perspectives on authority in the church.

The conversation across the church is shaping the direction of the church. A conversation about the authority of the teaching office is a conversation about the nature of the church. In relation to the nature of authority the church has to ask what is most appropriate in the light of its heritage and spirit, as well as what kind of church it will become. The answers to these questions will affect the character of its educational ministry. The nature of the conversation as it has taken shape recently has often included the conviction that the purpose of religious education is *identity construction,* meaning that the ''education endeavor'' of a ''religious community is to nurture in individuals the formation of a unique and distinctive identity, one which faithfully represents the integrity and historical roots of the community of which it is a member.''[5]

It is possible that this direction could lead to exclusive parochialism. However, a consciousness of identity need not necessarily lead in that direction. Identity consciousness can open persons to true inclusiveness, for it is ''in possessing our own particularity that we come to feel at home with ourselves and are best able to enter communion with others, freely giving and receiving of each other.''[6]

The early church faced a similar situation, which required that the disciples be formed and equipped for life amid cultural and religious pluralism. The Gospels were clearly the work of teachers setting forth in dynamic narrative and witness what was to be taught. Out of great diversity among texts, traditions, and world views, the canon served to specify the core of Christian belief and to ensure ''right teaching.'' The Councils hammered out parameters for the faith, identifying heresies and articulating the core of Christian belief through the Creeds.

Historically, the teaching office of the church was influenced by Jewish roots and the legacy of Jesus, who was called teacher:

"He taught them as one having authority, and not as their scribes" (Matt. 7:29). The Gospels record the question posed to Jesus by the priests and elders: "By what authority are you doing these things, and who gave you this authority?" (Matt. 21:23b). The teaching office took shape in the experience of the first-century church. Early congregations honored the office of teaching. Gifted people were charged to teach young converts. Gradually the office received exalted status, with apostles regarded as authoritative teachers who instructed others. "Teachers like Timothy (I Tim. 4:11-16) set a model, which in due course became taken up into the office of [bishop], so that in the pre-Nicene church (before A.D. 325), the bishop was essentially a 'prophet-teacher.' "[7]

Early in the tradition, authoritative teaching was invested in the ordained clergy. This continued during the Middle Ages as clergy decided which beliefs and practices were correct, meeting any opposition with the threat of excommunication, inquisition, and physical torture. The Protestant Reformation shifted teaching authority away from ecclesial authority with the pronouncement that grace and the love of God come to all directly through Christ. The function of right teaching was to keep that doctrinal clarity. Pietism encouraged persons to interpret Scripture for themselves without clergy assistance.[8]

Since Methodism was not confessional in nature, nor did it have its beginning in theological or doctrinal debate, the issue of the teaching office, especially the idea of a *magisterium,* did not achieve prominence. Methodism did not regard established standards of doctrine literally or juridically. It did not act out of a claim that the essence of Christian truth ought to be stated in precisely defined propositions, legally enforced by ecclesiastical authority. Rather, Methodists have turned to a conciliar model dependent on the collective wisdom demonstrated in the Conference. The questions of authority in teaching were present at the earliest of Wesley's conferences. The following three questions composed the agenda of that first conference: What to teach? How to teach? What to do?[9]

The spirit of the Conference, as well as these questions, is still present today. The teaching office as a function of the ministry of the church includes in its definition a wide range of authority issues. Who shall teach? Where shall teaching occur? What shall be taught? How shall it be taught?

Our twentieth-century world has been characterized as having a "homelessness of mind" that calls for renewed attention to the human need for clarity about belief and meaning. This attitude has affected the conversation on the authority of teaching in The United Methodist Church. The mood reflects the opinion of many that

> We need to be more deliberate in our approach to helping persons claim the Christian inheritance in such a way that they can come to know who they are and why they are. Teaching, then, as an intentional activity, may be employed as an instrument for use by the church in helping persons find meaning in a chaotic world.[10]

We hope this book can serve to stimulate the continuing conversation in the church over the authority of teaching. We have designed the book to engage individuals and groups in exploring who should teach, what should be taught, and how it should be taught in The United Methodist Church. It is intended to help clarify what is central in a United Methodist approach to educational ministry. Our invitation to participate in the conversation is to all: pastors, directors of Christian education, theological school faculty and students, bishops, district superintendents, conference and national staff members, editors and curriculum writers, and church lay leaders and teachers.

The book is divided into four parts. The first part is introductory. The second explores "Conversations from the

Past'' that influence our contemporary discussions. The third identifies ''Guidelines for Contemporary Conversations on Teaching'' to be found in *The Book of Discipline* and General Conference actions. The last section lifts up ''Voices That Need to Be Heard'' from those who have usually been on the margins of church decisions about teaching and from those engaged in educational research and writing.

An introduction to each section of the book provides an overview and a set of questions to enable understanding, dialogue, and further conversation. We hope these questions will lead to further dialogue and discussion, reflection, and action. The challenge is to discover what is necessary and called for in the teaching ministry of the church that can contribute to an authentic presentation of the gospel and the call to discipleship. The conversation can have a decisive effect on the assumptions, content, method, and approach of education for local churches in the future in order that the church may authoritatively proclaim another two hundred years of grace and freedom.

NOTES

1. Allen Moore, ''Toward a Theology of Christian Education for the 1980s,'' Prepared at the request of the Department of Church School Development of the General Board of Discipleship of The United Methodist Church (Unpublished, March 15, 1978), p. 3.

2. David Tracy, *Plurality and Ambiguity* (San Francisco: Harper & Row, 1987), p. 90.

3. See *The Daily Christian Advocate* (May 2, 1988): 252.

4. Richard Wilke, *And Are We Yet Alive?* (Nashville: Abingdon Press, 1986), see especially pp. 11-28.

5. Donald Miller, "Religious Education and Cultural Pluralism," *Religious Education* 74, 4 (July–August 1979): 339-49.

6. Constance J. Tarasar, "Educating for Identity and Openness," in *Religious Pluralism and Religious Education,* ed. Norma H. Thompson (Birmingham: Religious Education Press, 1988), p. 202.

7. William H. Gentz, gen. ed., *The Dictionary of Bible and Religion* (Nashville: Abingdon Press, 1986), p. 1027.

8. See Don E. Miller, *Story and Content* (Nashville: Abingdon Press, 1987), pp. 130-32; Howard Grimes, "Authority," in *The Westminster Dictionary of Christian Education,* Kendig Brubacher Cully and Iris V. Cully, eds. (Philadelphia: Westminster Press, 1968), pp. 42-44; Howard Grimes, "Church Education: A Historical Survey and a Look to the Future," *Perkins Journal* (Spring 1972): 19-38.

9. See *The Book of Discipline of The United Methodist Church* (Nashville: The United Methodist Publishing House, 1984), pp. 40-41.

10. Sara Little, *To Set One's Heart* (Atlanta: John Knox Press, 1983), p. 5.

II.
CONVERSATIONS FROM THE PAST

The contemporary discussions of teaching authority have been shaped by the conversations of the past. In the two chapters that follow, Richard Robert Osmer and Thomas A. Langford identify central themes and major concerns in the conversations among the Protestant Reformers and early Methodists. Both writers discern important clues in the past for authoritative teaching in the present. We offer the following questions to guide your own assessment of their analysis of the church's teaching heritage.

1. In what ways are the three primary tasks of the teaching office still central to the church's teaching today?

2. At what points are Luther's and Calvin's understanding of the teaching office relevant to contemporary United Methodist practices in teaching?

3. If a conciliar understanding of authority is taken seriously today, who would need to participate in decisions about what, who, and how United Methodists should teach?

4. What are the strengths and problems in a conciliar view of authority, given the social, political, and economic realities of contemporary life and church structure?

5. What are the strengths and problems in the proposals Osmer and Langford make to reclaim the teaching office today?

Chapter 2

Teaching in the Reformed Tradition:
The Contribution of Luther and Calvin

Richard Robert Osmer

Seeking a Third Way

The shifting landscape of religious America has created many problems for mainline Protestant denominations: a precipitous decline in membership, uncertainty about how to cope in a genuinely pluralistic society, and widespread ambivalence toward the old civic faith, to name but a few.[1] In the face of this situation, many in the mainline Protestant churches have begun to ask themselves where they went wrong. Some have sought answers in quick-fix church growth programs. Others have turned to approaches designed to return to the "spiritual" religion of an earlier era. Most have overlooked the important role that failures in the teaching office of these churches have played in their problems. And few have any awareness of the ways that their Reformation heritage might point them in directions that would be helpful in rectifying the failures of their teaching ministry.

This chapter represents an attempt to open the question of the teaching office in mainline Protestantism for discussion. It argues that Martin Luther and John Calvin developed a theological understanding of the teaching ministry surprisingly relevant to the challenges currently before these churches. It contends the Reformers' thought may help these churches clarify the unique contribution they have to make to the emerging religious America. It points to a perspective beyond modern individualism and countermodern authoritarianism that profoundly influences contemporary mainline Protestant churches and American culture.[2]

The difficulties posed by modern individualism have received eloquent expression in the widely influential book *Habits of the Heart*.[3] Robert Bellah and his colleagues argue convincingly that modern individualism has become the "first" moral language of many Americans. Whether appealing to the cost/benefit calculation of a utilitarian individualism or the emotivism of an expressive individualism, this cultural tradition undercuts the authority of the church's teaching office. Any sense that the church's teachings have priority over the individual in the determination of beliefs and moral commitments is lost when the individual is made the arbiter of life's meaning and purpose. A revitalized teaching office in the church today faces the task of overcoming precisely the rampant influence of this kind of individualism within Protestantism.

To recognize the threat of modern individualism to the mainline Protestant churches is not enough, however. Equally dangerous is the lure of countermodernizing forces. Increasingly, sociologists identify groups that explicitly define themselves as being over against certain features of modern life.[4] If modernization brings about a certain degree of cultural pluralism, for example, countermodernizing groups advocate the exclusive authority of the one true faith they espouse. Of particular concern is the tendency of countermodernizing groups toward authoritarianism: the demand for submission to beliefs and practices on the basis of an absolute religious authority that cannot be questioned. Peter Berger and others have pointed out the fact that this usually creates a defensive posture in such groups.[5] Against challenges posed by modernity, they reassert traditional authority with a force and certainty it did not originally possess.

According to the research of sociologist James Hunter, evangelical Christianity represents the most influential countermodernizing force in contemporary America, especially in its fundamentalist forms.[6] At the doctrinal level, it has viewed itself as the guardian of Protestant orthodoxy.[7] At the sociomoral level, it has repeatedly attempted to reassert traditional forms of authority in the areas of human sexuality, the family, and civic life.[8] While Hunter's thesis would take far more time to elaborate than we have in this chapter, it points to important problems that emerge when this perspective serves as the foundation of the church's teaching office. In the attempt to reaffirm traditional forms of authority, it denies the ways that the church's teachings are mediated through history, necessitating an ongoing process of interpretation for new times and contexts. It also leads to a diminished capacity for self-criticism based on an awareness that the church's teachings are always fallible and subject to correction.

Neither modern individualism nor countermodern authoritarianism provides an adequate foundation for the teaching office in the mainline Protestant churches. The teaching office as it is portrayed in the thought of the great Reformers represents a third perspective for understanding the authority and function of the church's teaching. While not abandoning individuals to their own resources in determining the central beliefs and practices of Christianity, it does not lapse into a form of authoritarianism. As the mainline churches struggle to discover the unique contribution they have to make to the new religious America, they would do well to rediscover the richness of this heritage.

The Teaching Office Defined

Before proceeding to our examination of the thought of Luther and Calvin on this topic, we must first pause and examine the terms *teaching office*.[9] This is no small matter and is worthy of extended reflection in its own right. Some of the most interesting research on this topic has been undertaken by Roman Catholic scholars, an outgrowth of the recent debate in that church over the nature and purpose of the *magisterium*.[10] The term *office* comes from the Latin *officium,* which originally referred to a wide variety of things: duty, service, function, business, place, and appointment. Of these many meanings, two have been appropriated by theology. First, *office* can be used to refer to the *function* that something carries out. For instance, we might say: "It is the office of an elevator to carry persons up and down a building" or "It is the office of the stomach to digest food." The emphasis here is on the function something plays and the various *tasks and responsibilities* that make up that function.

In the second usage, *office* refers to the position or *institutional role* to which a particular function is attached. For example, we might say: "The office of the chairperson of the finance committee is charged with convening that committee and making sure it composes a budget for the church." Here, emphasis highlights a specific role in an institution that has certain rights and responsibilities attached to it.

Throughout this chapter, the term *office* will refer primarily to the first of these uses. "Teaching office" points toward the *teaching function* of the church. It is one of the church's ministries and is a part of its *esse,* or being. As a function, however, it requires certain institutional roles or agencies. The church's teaching ministry necessarily takes institutional form.

It is important to distinguish between teaching function and institutional role, however, and to assign priority to the former. The teaching function has been carried out in a variety of forms across the centuries. Roman Catholic scholars have been particularly insistent on this historical fact in recent years in an effort to get some leverage on the monarchical papalist model of the teaching office that has been in ascendancy in the Roman Catholic church in the modern era.[11] Mainline Protestantism, however, still faces the important task of formulating structures, roles, and processes—in short, a form—appropriate to the teaching office in a denominational pattern of church life.

What are the tasks and responsibilities that make up the teaching function? They emerge out of the early history of the church and represent functional requirements of the church as a teaching community. It is not possible to extrapolate the church's teaching ministry directly from Jesus' own life and work, due to the virtual impossibility of identifying a special teaching ministry clearly distinguishable from Jesus' preaching, acts of healing, and other dimensions of his public ministry.[12] Only as the church began to organize itself as a community did various ministerial functions and roles begin to be clearly distinguished.

Two factors significantly influenced the emergence of the teaching office: the passing of the original generation of apostles and the rapid expansion of the church into non-Jewish cultural settings. With the death of those who had been eyewitnesses of Jesus' ministry, an authority vacuum emerged in the church's life.[13] In the face of competing understandings of Christianity, how could continuity with the original message of Jesus and the apostolic church be maintained? No longer could an appeal be made to eyewitnesses. The church now began to develop structures and roles to maintain continuity with the past in its teaching.

Similarly, the delay of the parousia and the penetration of the church into the Gentile world required new interpretations of the faith.[14] The Jewish eschatological framework presupposed by Jesus and the early church began to give way to one centered

31

on Christology, focusing on the person and nature of Christ in relation to the Godhead.[15] The church consequently developed teachings meaningful to persons whose world view differed significantly from that of Christians coming from a Jewish background.

The church, during the first centuries of its life, thus faced the tasks of preserving continuity with the original message of Jesus and the apostolic church while reinterpreting this message in shifting cultural contexts. A variety of structures and roles began to emerge at various levels of church life to carry out this ministry.[16] General councils were convened to define the official teachings of the church in the face of conflicting theological positions. The office of bishop gradually came to be granted a variety of responsibilities for teaching and preserving the faith in the areas under its jurisdiction. Various forms of catechetical instruction began to serve as an important way of shaping the dispositions and attitudes of converts and providing them with a common set of teachings. In short, the church became self-conscious about its teaching office and began to devise structures, roles, and processes that were specifically designed to carry out this ministry.

While the form of the teaching office has varied across the centuries, three tasks have consistently characterized this ministry. These tasks represent functional imperatives of the church as a teaching community. They include: (1) a determination of the normative beliefs and practices of the church; (2) the ongoing reinterpretation of these beliefs and practices in the face of shifting historical and cultural contexts; and (3) the formation and sustenance of educational institutions, processes, and curricula by which the church's beliefs and practices are taught, allowing them to be appropriated meaningfully by each new generation and grasped with deeper understanding over the course of an individual's life.

A few comments about each of these tasks are in order before we proceed to Luther and Calvin. The first task of the teaching office—the determination of the church's normative beliefs and practices—focuses on the activity of setting forth those teachings by which the church identifies itself as a community.[17] In large part, this involves the transmission and preservation of the core elements of the heritage of a church community, those items upon which its identity is based. Historically, this has been closely linked to the teaching ministry in a manner that goes far beyond the way we typically think of this ministry in the contemporary church.

By definition, every community is bound together by a complex set of social definitions, norms, and practices by which its members can interpret the world and act in it.[18] These beliefs and practices allow community members to interpret both what the world *is* and what it *ought* to be.[19] As such, they are normative. Frequently, these norms and definitions are transmitted and transformed through predominantly unconscious processes, such as socialization or the ordinary interactions of everyday life.

At certain times, however, communities attempt to lift up and give specification to the normative beliefs and practices that constitute and distinguish them. This often occurs when the identity of a community is threatened. In the first centuries of the church's life, for example, general councils were convened in the face of widespread disagreement and turmoil to define the theological positions that maintained genuine continuity with the message of Jesus and the apostolic church. These decisions constituted the official teachings of the church.

Such explicit definition of the normative beliefs and practices of a community, however, does not take place only during times of crisis. It also occurs in conjunction with the projection of the *paideia* informing the educational efforts of a given community. The term *paideia* comes from Greek culture and represents the self-conscious ideals of human good and excellence, which determine how a society educates its members.[20] Under the impress of its *paideia,* a community decides the substance and the process of its educational activities.

Across the centuries, the church's determination of its normative beliefs and practices has taken place in conjunction with the Christian *paideia* informing its educational activities at any given time. Declaratory creeds used in baptismal services during the first century, and catechetical instruction for example, reflected the community's consensus about the beliefs necessary to a proper cognitive apprehensive of the God of Christianity.[21] They functioned as part of the self-conscious ideal or *paideia* by which the church educated its members. Throughout church history, initiation into the normative expressions of the past, as expressed in catechisms, creeds, liturgy, and behavioral norms, has been an important focal point of the first task of the teaching office: to provide continuity with the original message of Jesus and the communion of saints through the ages.

The "determination" of the normative beliefs and practices of the church at any given time, however, involves more than simple transmission. The teaching office never merely repeats the past in the present. It uses the inherited tradition as a way of formulating normative statements of faith and moral guidelines for today's church. The tradition is preserved by extending it into the present. This brings us to the second task of the teaching office, the ongoing reinterpretation of the church's normative beliefs and practices in the face of shifting cultural and historical contexts.

It would be false to distinguish this task too sharply from the one just described. The transmission of the church's past is always selective, involving an interpretive process. The task of reinterpretation, however, is important in its own right. From the beginning, the mainstream of Christianity has attempted to be "catholic," relating its particular faith in Jesus Christ to all races, cultures, and eras and striving to be more than a self-enclosed sect. This has involved the church in a process of ongoing reinterpretation of the faith. It has addressed issues, used languages, and formed patterns of life that were not explicitly a part of the original message of Jesus and the apostolic church. As it has attempted to teach and preach the gospel ''once delivered,'' it has recognized that it can only truly do so by taking the risks inherent in addressing the sins, needs, and circumstances of its own day.

At various points in the church's history, the reinterpretive task of the church's teaching office has stood in tension with its effort to transmit and determine the normative expressions of the community's faith. Reinterpretation frequently involves stretching the inherited tradition in ways that seem to threaten continuity with the past. Innovation in such things as theological language, worship, and social relationships may appear to deviate from normative expressions of the faith that serve as important foci for the community's identity. The recent effort by feminist theologians to rethink important dimensions of the Christian faith illustrates the sort of genuine challenge that the ongoing process of interpretation in the teaching office can pose. Other modern challenges have ranged from an awareness of historical consciousness to the struggle for liberation in many Third World countries. The need to engage in the ongoing interpretation of the faith in shifting cultural context, however, has existed from the very beginning of the church's life. In this regard, Scripture itself establishes the pattern of interpretation and reinterpretation of traditions (e.g., the covenant) in response to emergent circumstances.

Frequently certain offices or agencies in the church focus their attention either on the first or second task of the teaching office. Theologians, for example, may engage in interpretations of the faith that go far beyond what the ordinary believer is ready to accept, pressing the church to come to grips with

contemporary insights. Representative bodies or denominational leaders, like bishops, on the other hand, may focus more of
their energy on maintaining continuity with the past, concerned
with sustaining communal identity in the face of social change.
The teaching office, however, must embrace the tensions that
frequently emerge as a result of these different emphases.
Without ongoing interpretation, the church too easily lapses
into an irrelevant, defensive orthodoxy. Without conservation
of the church's past and concern for its norms, the church loses
its sense of identity and overaccommodates the spirit of the age.
At its best, the teaching office finds ways of carrying out both of
these tasks.

The third task of the teaching office involves the formation
and sustenance of educational institutions, processes, and
curricula by which the church's beliefs and practices are taught,
allowing them to be appropriated meaningfully by each new
generation and grasped with deeper understanding over the
course of an individual's life. The teaching office of the church
includes more than educational institutions and material. When
a representative body of a denomination struggles to formulate
moral guidelines on a contemporary social issue, for example,
the teaching office is at work. The church, however, must
formulate special institutions, processes, and material designed
specifically to teach the faith.

It is helpful, I believe, to distinguish conceptually two key
terms at this point: *education* and *teaching*. *Education* refers to
ongoing structures and patterns *on the level of the community*.
Teaching focuses on *specific occasions* within educational
institutions and processes and attempts *to foster learning and
deepened understanding* of a particular subject matter.[22]

A more precise definition of *education* can be given as
follows: Education is a community's systematic and intentional
efforts to transmit and evoke knowledge, attitudes, values, and
skills that are deemed worthwhile.[23] It is a community's right

and obligation to be self-conscious about those items that it deems worthwhile and worthy of inclusion in its educational activities. Typically, such items represent a body of complex, interrelated information, skills, and attitudes that must be learned, necessitating the systematic and intentional organization of institutions, material, and persons into an unfolding course of study over time. This traditionally has been referred to as an educational curriculum.

Education, as it is being used here, focuses on a *communal* level. *Teaching,* in contrast, takes place within ongoing educational patterns. It occurs when persons gather together with the purpose of deepening their understanding of a particular subject matter. While a community has the right to determine its normative beliefs and practices, when it comes to the actual event of teaching, these must be brought to bear in such a way as to enhance the *understanding* of the learner, based on his or her capacities and desire to learn. Understanding here means much more than cognitive apprehension. It encompasses a gestalt of thought, emotion, and behavior for the construction and expression of meaning. Teaching, in that it is oriented toward the enhancement of understanding, can be distinguished from indoctrination.[24] It assumes respect for the learner; it attempts to foster the learner's construction of meaning. With this perspective on teaching, the authority proper to the teaching office is based on its ability to engage persons in a learning process, directing their attention to certain ideas, issues, or moral imperatives in ways that deepen or transform their prior understanding. It does not demand blind obedience, but engages in persuasion. Its authority resides in its perceived competence and wisdom, resting on the freely given respect of the learner. When the teaching office of the church loses contact with teaching in this sense, substituting its juridical power for a genuine attempt to enhance understanding, then it has lost its reason for being. It is precisely this loss that led the great Reformers to engage in a life and death struggle with the Roman Catholic *magisterium* of their day.

The Teaching Office in Luther's and Calvin's Thought

It was inevitable that Martin Luther and John Calvin would confront the question of the church's teaching office in their conflict with Rome. Far more than is commonly realized, the Reformation was fought over the quo of magisterial authority (the "who" of the teaching office) as well as the quid (the "what" of its teachings). This may surprise many contemporary Protestants whose understanding of the Reformers' views of the church's teaching authority is badly distorted.

One piece of Reformation history typifies this widespread distortion in contemporary Protestantism. It centers on Luther's closing remarks at the Diet of Worms in 1521. Having already been excommunicated by the pope and his teachings condemned by the University of Paris, Luther was called before the Diet by Emperor Charles V to give account of his position. He was allowed to answer only two questions put to him: Did he acknowledge the books published under his name as his own? Did he stand by their content or wish to recant?

At the forceful conclusion of his response, Luther replied:

> Unless I am overcome by the testimony of Scripture or by clear reason (for I believe neither the pope nor councils by themselves), I remain conquered by the Scriptures which I have adduced. As long as my conscience is captive to the words of God, I neither can nor will recant, since it is neither safe nor right to act against conscience. God help me. Amen.[25]

Luther's appeal to conscience here would seem virtually identical to the understanding of the church's teaching authority held by many contemporary Protestants. Did he not argue that individual conscience is to reign supreme, that it is more authoritative than any ecclesiastical structure, including specially designated leaders, councils, and denominational doctrinal standards? Do not persons stand in an unmediated relationship to God, with salvation essentially a transaction between the individual and God? Is not private interpretation of Scripture the right of every individual believer?

This highly individualistic understanding of the Christian life, however, has more to do with the contemporary church than with Luther. While individual conscience does have an important role in Luther's thought (and in Calvin's as well), it is only one of a cluster of authorities in the Christian life, all of which are subordinate to and derivative of the authority of the gospel. In the passage quoted above, Luther's appeal to conscience is not primarily an appeal to the authority of the Spirit-filled individual over against the religious establishment. Neither is it based on the natural rights of the individual vis-à-vis society. Rather, it rests on the authority of Scripture as it witnesses to the gospel, an authority that transcends every human institution or tradition. On this foundation, Luther and Calvin built their understandings of the church's teaching office. While there are real differences between these two men, common themes in their understanding of the teaching office can be identified. Our approach will be to treat them together, attempting to sketch the general contours of the teaching office given classical expression in their thought.

At the heart of the great Reformers' theologies was an affirmation of the absolute priority of the gospel.[26] The good news of God's gratuitous mercy revealed in Jesus Christ stands at the beginning and the end of the Christian life. Humanity exists in rebellion against God and can be restored to a relationship with its Maker only through the forgiveness won in the life, death, and resurrection of the Mediator, Jesus Christ. The foundation of the Christian life, thus, is the unmerited, alien righteousness freely given to a sinful humanity in Jesus Christ. The gospel authoritatively teaches humanity who God is and who human beings are in relation to God and one another. The gospel is the authority above all authorities in the church, the foundation upon which all others rest.

Second in importance in the Reformers' thought is the authority of Scripture.[27] Scripture contains the accounts of the original apostolic witness to Jesus Christ. As such, it stands in a closer relationship to the source of faith than any other authority in the church. All matters of faith and morality necessary to salvation are contained in its teachings. The authority of Scripture, however, is subordinate to that of the gospel. The good news of God's gratuitous mercy in Jesus Christ represents the center of Scripture and is the means by which all other parts are interpreted. Luther was far freer than Calvin in his acknowledgment of a canon within the canon and his willingness to weigh and judge the relative value of other parts of Scripture by this hermeneutical key. However, Calvin also advocated a Christocentric interpretation of Scripture, arguing that the triune God revealed in Jesus Christ was the same God found in the law and the prophets.

Neither man identified the words of the Bible with the gospel in a straightforward manner.[28] Moreover, both understood Scripture's authority primarily in terms of how it functions as a mediator of saving truth. Its role is to enable the proclamation of the gospel from age to age. It is not primarily a source book of infallible theological propositions that have a timeless quality. Its witness to Christ enables living witnesses to proclaim the gospel in their own time and place.

An important part of both men's thought was their binding of the Holy Spirit to Scripture. The Spirit *attests* to the saving truth of Scripture, and Scripture *tests* the operation of the Holy Spirit.[29] The former refers to the belief that the inner witness of the Spirit is the only way that the gospel of Scripture can become saving truth for any individual. Faith can never be merely a matter of assent to the church's external authority and the articles of faith it defines. It ultimately rests on God's action in the Spirit, which attests to the forgiveness won in Christ and witnessed to by Scripture. The latter is equally important. Scripture tests the Spirit in the sense that every claim of the Spirit's presence must be tested by the teachings of the Bible. Those who claim to speak on the Spirit's behalf must appeal to the written Word. This is as true of charismatic leaders as it is of members of the church hierarchy. The Spirit is not bound in a mechanical fashion to particular offices or gatherings of the church, nor is it the free property of any individual who has a particular kind of religious experience. It is bound to the written Word.

Upon the foundation of the gospel and Scripture the ministry of the church, including the teaching office, is erected in the Reformers' thought. The primary function of the teaching office witnesses to the saving truth of the gospel and enables the new life in Christ, which it brings. *The teaching office of the church does not determine the gospel as revealed in Scripture; it is determined by it.* The preaching of the gospel called the church into being and determines its life and mission. In the Reformers' view, the manifest witness of Scripture to the gospel, must remain the norm of norms in the church. It contains all that is necessary for salvation. As theologians would put it later, it is "sufficient." No dogma or practice formulated by the church's teaching office possesses this kind of authority. The church's teachings are subordinate to and in the service of the gospel of forgiveness and the new life that it brings.

This affirmation of the unique authority of the gospel as witnessed to by Scripture brought Luther and Calvin into conflict with the teaching office of their day. The *magisterium* of the church, they argued, sets itself above Scripture, claiming the authority of the Holy Spirit in formulating articles of faith and practice. In this way, the traditions of the church are placed

41

on an equal footing with the Bible. Such an understanding of the teaching office was vehemently rejected. As Calvin puts it in the *Institutes*:

> If we grant the first point, that the church cannot err in matters necessary to salvation, here is what we mean by it: The statement is true in so far as the church, having forsaken all its own wisdom, allows itself to be taught by the Holy Spirit through God's Word. This, then, is the difference. Our opponents locate the authority of the church outside God's Word; but we insist that it be attached to the Word, and do not allow it to be separated from it.[30]

Does this mean that the teaching office of the church is reduced to repeating the words of the Bible in a mechanical fashion? Does this rule out a role for church tradition and ecclesiastical authorities in the ongoing interpretation of Scripture from age to age? The answer to these questions is an unequivocal no. The Reformers' emphasis on the authority of the gospel and Scripture, however, does mean that all other authorities by which the church carries out its teaching ministry are *humanized*. None can claim the absolute authority that can be accorded the gospel and Scripture alone. Teaching authorities are human—finite, even sinful, agencies of the church. They are fallible and subject to correction.

Moreover, the Reformers' strong affirmation of the authority of the gospel and Scripture led them to advocate a particular form of the teaching office. A highly centralized, hierarchical form of the teaching office, they believed, inevitably tempts the leaders of the church to substitute their own teachings for those of Christ. This is precisely the criticism that Luther and Calvin made against the *magisterium* of their day. The form of the teaching office they advocated granted important roles to multiple offices and agencies scattered throughout the church.

The Reformers perhaps can best be described as advocating a *dialogical model of the teaching office*.

No single authority can lay exclusive claim to the definitive conservation and interpretation of Scripture. As each attempts to do so, it must confront other authorities in the church, which can correct, expand, or confirm its understanding of Christian teaching. Each must base its authority on the conformity of its teachings to the gospel as witnessed in Scripture. Out of the ongoing conversation between multiple penultimate teaching authorities, normative beliefs and practices of the church are determined and reinterpreted.

It is not possible in the space of this paper to develop in any depth an examination of even one of the teaching authorities the Reformers advocated. However, we can provide some insight into the sorts of offices and agencies at various levels of the church's life that played important roles in the teaching office as they understood it.

Both Reformers valued the significant role *representative bodies* played in determining the normative beliefs and practices of the church and in carrying out their ongoing reinterpretation. Church councils, for example, played a particularly important role in their thought. Both accepted the authority of the ecumenical councils of the first centuries, which defined the doctrines of the Trinity and the twofold nature of Christ. They accepted the teachings of these councils, however, not because of their authority as councils per se, but because what they taught was thought to be in conformity with the basic substance of Scripture.

At certain points, Luther and Calvin were even willing to quibble over the language of these councils. As teaching authorities, they were fallible human agencies, subject to Scripture and the gospel. Their twofold task included: (1) providing continuity with the message of Jesus and the apostolic church by setting forth articles of faith in terms intelligible to persons in a particular time and place, and (2) settling doctrinal disputes. As Calvin puts it in the *Institutes*:

> We indeed willingly concede, if any discussion arises over doctrine, that the best and surest remedy is for a synod of true bishops to be convened, where the doctrine at issue may be examined. Such a definition, upon which the pastors of the church in common, invoking Christ's Spirit, agree, will have much more weight than if each one, having conceived it separately at home, should teach it to the people, or if a few private individuals should compose it.[31]

This view balanced an equally strong affirmation of the need to subject the teachings of councils to the scrutiny of other authorities in the church. As Calvin goes on to write:

> But whenever a decree of any council is brought forward, I should like men first of all diligently to ponder at what time it was held, on what issue, and with what intention, what sort of men were present; then to examine by the standard of Scripture what it dealt with—and to do this in such a way that the definition of the council may have its weight and be like a provisional judgment, yet not hinder the examination which I have mentioned.[32]

This critical appreciation of the role of church councils in the teaching office has continued to play an important role in the life of churches standing in the Reformation heritage. Both the Lutheran and Reformed traditions, for example, have viewed the confessions formed by representative bodies as having a kind of normative status in the church. They are not infallible statements. They are subject to correction and revision, but they do represent the church's effort to confess what it believes in a particular time and place.

Frequently, such confessions have given rise to official catechisms, which also have been subjected to the critical review of representative bodies. Such catechisms represent a direct link between the teachings formulated by representative bodies and the ongoing education taking place in congregations. Both Luther and Calvin advocated such "set formularies" of the faith as a way of introducing all Christians to the basic teachings of Scripture and affording a measure of unity in the church. In addition to the framing of normative statements of belief in confessions and catechisms, Luther and Calvin also advocated a role for representative bodies in offering ongoing guidance to the church on social and moral issues of contemporary importance. Once more, such teachings were not seen as infallible or even binding on members of the church. But they did represent an important source of guidance for individuals and congregations as they struggled to discern God's will for their lives. This sort of teaching by representative bodies continues in the social policy statements of such denominational agencies as the General Assembly of the Presbyterian Church (U.S.A.), the General Conference of The United Methodist Church, and other gatherings of representatives of the church.

Another locus of teaching in the church existed in the ongoing work of theologians. Both Luther and Calvin viewed their own theological work as an attempt to measure the contemporary beliefs and practices of the church against the teachings of Scripture. Neither felt bound in a slavish fashion to the inherited traditions of the church. The theologian must first and foremost be committed to the question of truth as it is posed by the gospel and Scripture. Indeed, Luther viewed his criticism of the papacy as a responsibility that grew out of his office as a doctor of the church, called to nurture the faith and life of the people of God through the teaching of the gospel.[33]

Theologians, as such, were not placed in a subordinate position to pastoral leaders, who were thought to possess supreme teaching authority. Nor were they to sacrifice their

45

own original study of Scripture to preexistent doctrinal writings. Theologians were to retain a measure of freedom in relation to the pastoral authority of church leaders. It is no accident that Luther began his criticism of the papacy while a member of the theological faculty at Wittenberg. The freedom of theologians has frequently received an institutional base in centers of higher education.

Developments since the Reformers' time have increased the complexity of the role of theologians in the teaching office, as theology has been forced to incorporate the insights of modern forms of rationality. Many theologians in the contemporary situation feel they can best serve the question of truth by living in the tension between the church and its authorities and the scholarly community and its ongoing inquiry. Seminaries frequently embody this tension, attempting simultaneously to conserve by transmitting and transform by reinterpreting this tradition in conjunction with contemporary insights.

In a very real sense, thus, theologians play an important role in the teaching office. Mainline Protestantism currently faces the question regarding how it can facilitate genuine dialogue between this locus of teaching authority and other levels of the church's life. Since its location in the modern university, theology has been fractured into multiple disciplines of a highly specialized nature.[34] The interrelationship of these disciplines and their relation to the piety of the ordinary believer is no longer obvious. To retrieve the Reformers' dialogical model of the teaching office, a much stronger relationship between theology and the ongoing life of the contemporary church must be forged.

An equally important center of the teaching office in the Reformers' thought was the congregation. Both Luther and Calvin believed that the congregation had the right to "test" the teachings of its leaders, including those of its own pastor and the church hierarchy. Especially during the early phases of the

46

Reformation, when the newly emerging churches were faced with a transitional period in which Roman Catholic priests continued to hold jurisdiction in certain areas, Luther strongly affirmed the ability of congregations to judge church teaching for themselves. In one such situation in Leipzig, he wrote a pamphlet for the Christian population with the long title "That a Christian Assembly or Congregation Has the Right and Power to Judge All Teaching and To Call, Appoint, and Dismiss Teachers, Established and Proven by Scripture."

Drawing on I Thessalonians 5:22 ("But test everything; hold fast what is good"), Luther writes in this pamphlet:

> See, he does not desire any tenet or teaching to be obeyed unless it is heard, tested, and recognized as good by the congregation that hears it. For this testing is not the concern of the teachers; rather, the teachers must announce beforehand that one should test. So here too judgment is withdrawn from the teachers and given to the students among the Christians.[35]

A clear affirmation of the congregation's right to judge and test the teachings offered by other authorities in the church is seen here. However, Luther did not absolutize the congregation's right in this regard, especially if his thought as a whole is taken into account. His conflict with Karlstadt and the Peasants' War made him more cautious in affirming the ability of a single congregation to interpret Scripture for itself and to judge definitively the offerings of other authorities.[36] In other words, he was not a strict congregationalist. The congregation was one of a larger configuration of authorities engaging in an ongoing dialogue in the teaching office.

In part, the congregation's function reflects Luther's appreciation of the *sensus fidelium,* the sense of the faithful. In a manner somewhat different from Calvin's, Luther was willing to grant authority to beliefs and practices widely held across the centuries in the church, if they did not explicitly contradict

47

Scripture.[37] The piety of ordinary believers in congregations has long exerted an influence on the formation of the church's normative beliefs and practices. For example, the practice of Christians praying to Christ as God decisively influenced the Arian controversy in the early church, resulting in the official teaching of the full divinity of Christ. Luther drew on the sense of the faithful in his argument with the Anabaptists over infant baptism. Since Scripture gives no definitive guidance on this matter, he felt that the church must rely on the fact that infant baptism has been "practiced since the beginning of the church" and has been "accepted among all Christians in the whole world."[38]

The sense of the faithful, of course, exceeds the wisdom and piety of an individual congregation at any given time. It points to beliefs and practices that have been accepted by ordinary believers over a long period of time. As the Reformers clearly recognized, pious conviction alone is no measure of truth. It must be subjected to other critical tests. Nonetheless, the sense of the faithful does have a role in the teaching office, and congregational life does represent a partial expression of this sense, serving as both a test and a source of teaching in the church. The official teachings of the church and the formulations of theologians must be brought into dialogue with the faith and life of ordinary Christians. In such a dialogue, truth does not always exist on the side of church leaders or theologians. Once again, we see the Reformers calling the mainline churches to a fuller understanding of the teaching office than is currently in place.

A final brief word must be said about the liberty of the individual Christian and the role of conscience in the teaching office. By now, it should be apparent that the Reformers cannot be assimilated to modern individualism in any straightforward manner. Both Luther and Calvin placed the individual Christian amid multiple teaching authorities at various levels of the church's life. The individual is situated in a concrete fellowship of believers that is itself open to an ongoing interchange with the teachings of past and present representative bodies, the catholic sense of the church, and the scholarly work of theologians.

The Reformers developed their understandings of the role of individual conscience and the place of Christian liberty not to set believers free to determine their own beliefs and practices by themselves but to free them from the domination of a teaching office that they believed was substituting its own decrees and laws for the gospel. Faith in the gospel and obedience to God's will remain the hallmarks of true Christian freedom. Individual conscience is "captive to the words of God," as Luther put it in the quotation offered above.

The authority of Scripture and the gospel, however, frees the individual from the burden of human teachings that claim for themselves an authority they do not warrant. Along these lines, the Lutheran tradition has developed a distinction between those teachings of Scripture necessary for salvation and those beliefs and practices that are *adiaphora,* "things that make no difference" or "things neither commanded nor forbidden."[39] In the latter sphere, individual conscience is given more latitude. It faces issues, commitments, and decisions of importance, but not of ultimate importance. They are not matters upon which salvation depends. The church has the right and responsibility to teach on issues that are *adiaphora,* but it must do so with the clear recognition of the proper limits of its authority and allow individual conscience to have its say. If the teaching office has done its work, it has formed conscience to exercise its legitimate freedom in a proper manner.

There are special occasions, however, when individual conscience reverberates back through the other authorities of the teaching office more directly. These are times of crisis, when the church through its various agencies is thought to betray the gospel and the moral imperatives consistent with it.

Those who stand in the Reformation heritage must always hold before them the fact that the church can and does err, that individuals may have to defy the teachings of the church because their conscience is bound to the words of God. On behalf of God and, ultimately, on behalf of the church, the individual must dissent. While this sort of situation is an emergency one and does not represent the normal role of individual conscience in the teaching office, it is an important part of the Reformation heritage.

At crucial points in the church's life, the conscience of individuals or prophetic groups may well hold up to the church certain parts of Scripture or its own tradition that have been neglected or even repressed by the current teaching office. It may well be, moreover, that conscience will lead persons to reject certain parts of the inherited tradition on the basis of a commitment to the "new thing" that God is doing in the church. A teaching office that is truly Protestant must be willing to hear the prophets in its midst and to bring them into the dialogue by which the church teaches what it believes and what it must do. The teaching office is only one ministry in the church's life. Its restoration is essential to the future of the mainline Protestant churches. But it must never become an end in itself, claiming privileges and authority that belong to God alone. For this reason, God calls both prophets and teachers that each might make a contribution to the edification of the church and the glory of God.

NOTES

1. Throughout this chapter, I will be following Wade Roof and William McKinney's definition of mainline Christianity: "The

dominant, culturally established faiths held by the majority of Americans'' (*American Mainline Religion: Its Changing Shape and Future* [New Brunswick: Rutgers University Press, 1987], p. 6). Historically, the mainline Protestant churches have been primarily Protestant: Episcopalians, Congregationalists, Presbyterians, Methodists, Lutherans, Reformed, and Baptists of moderate persuasion. However, it is increasingly apparent that these churches are not dominant in the same way that they once were. Roof and McKinney go so far as to point out that ''old line'' may be a more accurate way of describing them. I use the term *mainline* primarily as a way of referring to these denominations because they have been willing to engage cultural issues across the centuries and have not set up tight boundaries in a sectarian fashion.

2. I have taken the term ''counter-modern'' from Peter Berger, Brigitte Berger, and Hansfried Kellner's book, *The Homeless Mind: Modernization and Consciousness* (New York: Vintage Books, 1973), chaps. 8–9. An important dimension of the conflict between the proponents of modern individualism and counter-modern authoritarianism is social location. Berger touches on this in a helpful way in ''From the Crisis of Religion to the Crisis of Secularity,'' in *Religion and America: Spirituality in a Secular Age,* eds. Mary Douglas and Steven Tipton (Boston: Beacon Press, 1982), pp. 19-24.

3. Robert Bellah, Richard Madsen, William Sullivan, Ann Swidler, and Steven Tipton, *Habits of the Heart: Individualism and Commitment in American Life* (Berkeley: University of California Press, 1985).

4. It is not hard to bring into mind examples of this world-wide phenomenon. The Shiite revolution in Iran represents an explicit rejection of the modernizing tendencies of the Shah. The astounding resurgence of indigenous religion and the parallel growth of the ''spiritual'' Christian churches in Africa also are examples of countermodernization at work.

5. I have found Peter Berger's discussion of the ''deductive possibility'' of religion in the face of modernization particularly helpful, although I believe that it is more applicable to contemporary evangelicalism than to Barth. See Peter Berger, *The Heretical*

Imperative: Contemporary Possibilities of Religious Affirmation (New York: Anchor Press, 1979), pp. 79-94.

6. See James Hunter, *American Evangelicalism: Conservative Religion and the Quandary of Modernity* (New Brunswick: Rutgers University Press, 1983); *Evangelicalism: The Coming Generation* (Chicago: University of Chicago Press, 1987). In both of these books, Hunter interprets evangelicalism sympathetically, attempting to show how it has withstood the "acids" of modernization. Clearly, I am offering a different evaluation of the "counter" position of evangelicalism. On theological grounds, I do not believe that a simple "countering" of modernity reflects the transforming relationship to culture to which the church is called. Moreover, this frequently has rendered evangelicalism unable to account for the ways that it has unconsciously incorporated certain features of modern life, a process that is inevitable and not necessarily evil.

7. Hunter, *Evangelicalism,* chap. 2.

8. Ibid., chaps. 3–5.

9. A more extended treatment may be found in Richard Robert Osmer, *A Teachable Spirit: Recovering the Teaching Office in Mainline Protestantism* (Louisville: Westminster/John Knox, 1990).

10. The literature on this topic is extensive. An excellent introduction to the *magisterium* by a moderate Roman Catholic is Francis Sullivan's *Magisterium: Teaching Authority in the Catholic Church* (Mahwah, N.J.: Paulist Press, 1983). Other books that serve as helpful introductions to the issues involved in the recent discussion among Catholics are Avery Dulles, *The Survival of Dogma* (New York: Crossroad, 1985); Hans Kung, *Infallible: An Inquiry,* trans. E. Quinn (New York: Doubleday & Co., 1983); John Kirvan, ed., *The Infallibility Debate* (New York: Paulist Press, 1971); Charles Curran and Richard McCormick, eds., *The Magisterium and Morality,* Readings in Moral Theology, no. 3 (New York: Paulist Press, 1982).

11. A particularly helpful overview of the different forms of the teaching office is Avery Dulles's article, "The *Magisterium* in History: A Theological Reflection," *Chicago Studies* 17, 2 (Summer 1978): 264-81. A particularly insightful discussion of the contempo-

rary conflict in the Roman Catholic Church is found in T. Howland Sanks, *Authority in the Church: A Study in Changing Paradigms* (American Academy of Religion, Dissertation Series, No. 2, 1974).

12. Robert Worley, *Preaching and Teaching in the Earliest Church* (Philadelphia: Westminster Press, 1967).

13. I follow Raymond Brown on this point. See Brown, *The Churches the Apostles Left Behind* (New York: Paulist Press, 1984) and Brown with John Meier, *Antioch and Rome: New Testament Cradles of Catholic Christianity* (London: Geoffrey Chapman, 1983).

14. Jaroslav Pelikan's account of this is particularly illuminating. See his *The Emergence of the Catholic Tradition (100-600),* The Christian Tradition I (Chicago: The University of Chicago Press, 1971).

15. See R. P. C. Hanson, *The Continuity of Christian Doctrine* (New York: Seabury Press, 1981), chap. 3.

16. A partial account can be found in James McCue and Arthur Piepkorn, "The Roman Primacy in the Patristic Era," in *Papal Primacy and the Universal Church: Lutherans and Catholics in Dialogue,* eds. Paul C. Empie and Thomas Austin Murphy (Minneapolis: Augsburg Press, 1974), pp. 43-97.

17. George Lindbeck, in describing the role of the normative convictions of every religion, observes: "These are those propositions which are essential to its identity and without which it would not be itself." *The Infallibility Debate,* ed. John Kirvan (New York: Paulist Press, 1971), p. 117.

18. Here, I locate myself in the "classical" sociological tradition of Max Weber and, to a lesser extent, Emile Durkheim.

19. Clifford Geertz, in *The Interpretation of Cultures* (New York: Basic Books, 1973), chaps. 4 and 5, provides a particularly good description of the *is* and *ought* to be of culture and religion.

20. Werner Jaeger's classic study of Greek *paideia* remains the definitive discussion of this concept. See his *Paideia: The Ideals of Greek Culture,* 3 vols. (New York: Oxford University Press, 1945). This concept has begun to reappear in recent discussions of theology and education. For example, see Edward Farley's use of it in his

Theologia: The Fragmentation and Unity of Theological Education (Philadelphia: Fortress Press, 1983), pp. 152-56, and James Fowler's in "Pluralism, Particularity, and Paideia," *The Journal of Law and Religion* II (1984): 263-307.

21. See J. N. D. Kelly, *Early Christian Creeds* (Essex, England: Longman Press, 1950), chap. 2.

22. My views on the importance of understanding in teaching have been influenced greatly by the thought of Charles Melchert and Sara Little. See Little's *To Set One's Heart: Belief and Teaching in the Church* (Atlanta: John Knox, 1983), pp. 23-25, and "Religious Instruction," in *Contemporary Approaches to Christian Education,* eds. Jack L. Seymour and Donald E. Miller (Nashville: Abingdon Press, 1982), pp. 43-45. Also, see Melchert's "Understanding and Religious Education," in *Process and Relationship,* eds. Iris V. Cully and Kendig Brubacher Cully (Birmingham, Ala.: Religious Education Press, 1978), pp. 41-48.

23. The influence of Lawrence Cremin's thought on this definition will be obvious to anyone familiar with his work. See his *Public Education* (New York: Basic Books, 1976), p. 27. More than Cremin, however, I want to call attention to the normative dimensions inherent in education. Hence, my use of the term *worthwhile.*

24. See Ronald Hynman's discussion in *Ways of Teaching* (New York: J.B. Lippincott, 1974), pp. 11-13.

25. Quoted in Scott Hendrix, *Luther and the Papacy: Stages in a Reformation Conflict* (Philadelphia: Fortress Press, 1981), p. 133.

26. Luther closely identifies the gospel with the doctrine of justification; at the heart of the good news that Christ brings is the forgiveness of sins offered to undeserving sinners. He describes the importance of this doctrine at various points as "the summary of Christian doctrine," "the sun which illuminates God's holy church," going so far as to write: "That on this article rests all that we teach and practice against the pope, the devil, and the world." (Paul Althaus, *The Theology of Martin Luther,* trans. Robert Schultz [Philadelphia: Fortress Press, 1966], p. 224.)

27. As Luther puts it at various points: "No authority after Christ is to

be equated with the apostles and the prophets''; ''Whatever they wish to teach or legislate, they ought to follow and accept the authority of the apostles''; ''All articles are sufficiently established in the Holy Scriptures, so that it is not necessary to establish any beyond these''; and ''Nothing in respect of either faith or morals can be established as necessary to salvation beyond what is taught in Scripture'' (quoted in Althaus, *Theology of Luther*, p. 5). Similarly, Calvin writes: ''But such wranglers are neatly refuted by just one word of the apostles. He testifies that the church is 'built upon the foundation of the prophets and the apostles' (Eph. 2:20). If the teaching of the prophets and apostles is the foundation, this must have had authority before the church began to exist'' (John Calvin, *Institutes of the Christian Religion*, vol. 1, ed. John T. McNeill, trans., Ford Lewis Battles [Philadelphia: Westminster Press, 1960], p. 75).

28. There is something of a debate among Calvin scholars on Calvin's understanding of Scripture in this regard. Edward Dowey, in *The Knowledge of God in Calvin's Theology* (New York: Columbia University Press, 1952), argues that Calvin subscribes to a dictation theory of inspiration (pp. 91ff). In contrast, persons like François Wendel and Donald McKim argue that he did not advocate a doctrine of biblical inerrancy on the basis of a high view of inspiration. See Wendel's *Calvin: The Origins and Development of His Religious Thought*, trans. Philip Mairet (New York: Harper & Row, 1963), p. 31, and Donald McKim, ed., ''Calvin's View of Scripture'' in *Readings in Calvin's Theology* (Grand Rapids: Baker Books, 1984), pp. 43-68.

29. Robert Johnson describes the relationship between the Spirit and Scripture in this way in *Authority in Protestant Theology* (Philadelphia: Westminster Press, 1959), pp. 54-56.

30. Calvin, *Institutes of the Christian Religion*, vol. 2, p. 1162.

31. Ibid., p. 1176.

32. Ibid., p. 1171.

33. Hendrix, *Luther and the Papacy*, p. 63.

34. Edward Farley's discussion of this is particularly important. See his *Theologia*.

35. Quoted in Gert Haendler, *Luther: On Ministerial Office and Congregational Function* (Philadelphia: Fortress Press, 1981), p. 59.

36. See Haendler's discussion of this in *Luther,* chaps. 6–8.

37. See Carl Braaten, *Principles of Lutheran Theology* (Philadelphia: Fortress Press, 1983), p. 10.

38. Quoted in Althaus, *Theology of Luther,* p. 359.

39. See Eric Gritsch, "Lutheran Teaching Authority: Past and Present," in *Teaching Authority and Infallibility in the Church—Lutherans and Catholics in Dialogue VI,* eds. Paul C. Empie, Thomas Austin Murphy, and Joseph A. Burgess (Minneapolis: Augsburg Publishing House, 1978), p. 138.

Chapter 3

Teaching in the Methodist Tradition:
A Wesleyan Perspective

Thomas A. Langford

How can a church that explicitly calls itself "apostolic" be sure it authentically presents the gospel it has received? How can a church maintain the truth of the gospel for its own life and for the sake of the world? These questions are central to the concerns of what has historically been called the teaching office of the church. In the pages that follow, we will examine a United Methodist response to these questions. Attention will be given to how The United Methodist Church understands its task in preserving the gospel, tests the church's proclamation and instruction, judges the church's life, assesses its interpretations, and establishes the criteria for its judgments. Implications will also be drawn regarding tasks confronting the church as it seeks to develop increasing clarity about its teaching responsibilities.

Let us begin our discussion with some historical observations. Methodism, as the Wesleyan revival movement, held theology to be inextricably joined with practice. To paraphrase Ludwig Wittgenstein: To have a theological language is to possess a form of life. The dominant implication of this conviction in Methodist history has been a type of pragmatism—truth is known in its application. Put differently, theology is to be judged by the quality of life it produces. Theology, in this tradition, has not been abstract, rather it has been understood predominantly as underwriting personal and communal spiritual and moral life. To know God is to love and serve God; truth about God is truth about life.

Such a norm has much to commend it. Nothing is more stultifying than self-certain and self-righteous rational orthodoxy, but this has not been Methodism's problem. Our problem has been the lack of clear authority for determining the interrelationship of theology with worship and moral life. We have been deficient in clarifying the grounding and testing of our praxis. We have been overbalanced toward action in contrast to reflection. As a result, Methodism has been too uncertain in its self-criticism and too prone to conform to non-theological (or non-distinctively Christian) influences and cultural values. Hence our actions are often primarily politically or sociologically or economically formed. This lack of clarity about the function of the teaching office in United Methodism has been influenced by the distinctive history of the church.

In John Wesley's time, annual conference meetings served as the *magisterium* of the Methodist Church. This represented a conciliarist approach to theological judgments and required the consensus of the community through its representatives. The role of Wesley was paramount and even imperious, but he acted within conference structure. This mode of theological consultation expressed Wesley's conviction that a Christian conference (in its several guises as band, class, or conference) can be a means of grace, and it continued to describe actual practice in Methodism. The supremacy of the conference as the "living Wesley" was maintained in British Methodism through conflict and challenge as expressed in the Leeds Organ Case (1820s), the Warrenite Secession (1834–35), and the Fly-Sheet Controversy (1849–53).

At the same time the attitude within Methodism toward the education of ordained ministers contributed to the failure to recognize a well-developed teaching office for preachers.[1] Both in England and in North America deep resistance hindered the organization of theological institutes and the formal education of pastors. In Great Britain, the Warrenite debates in the 1830s revealed strong anti-intellectualism. And in North America negative attitudes toward college-trained preachers (see for instance, Peter Cartwright's autobiography) resisted any educational program beyond the individualized course of study.[2] A lack of trust in explicit theological leadership was evident, along with a conservative attitude toward doctrinal formulations (note the restrictive rules in the *Discipline*). All these factors reinforced a hesitancy to engage in an ongoing and significant exercise of the teaching office. The General Conference retained power, but little will, to exercise the office except where pressed by political necessity (as with the issue of Christian holiness in the 1890s). Instead creative theological reflection focused, for the most part, on moral issues, as found in the Social Creed.

In North American Methodism, the General Conference functioned as the interpretative authority for the church. Polity, theology, and engagement with culture were intertwined, and in all these areas the General Conference was the authoritative voice of what was authentic, necessary, or allowable. In the breakup of the North American church in the 1840s new authoritative structures emerged. In the Methodist Episcopal Church, South, the Council of Bishops became the final court of appeal for all disciplinary matters. In the Methodist Episcopal Church, the General Conference retained its supreme position. In the 1939 union of these two churches with the Methodist Protestant Church, the creation of a Judicial Council established a compromise arbiter (superseding both the General Conference and the Council of Bishops) of what the *Discipline* means or what the will of the General Conference intends. More and more the interpretive authority of the Judicial Council has been exercised, for the most part, to maintain legitimate procedure and to adjudicate counter claims. It has not dealt directly with substantive theological issues. The General Conference can and does still exercise the power of theological interpretation, but usually indirectly and through discussion of particular issues of practice and polity.

In actual practice, a secondary, but pervasive, set of influences on the church's teaching is to be found in some of the boards and agencies, such as the Board of Discipleship, the Board of Global Ministries, and The United Methodist Publishing House, with its responsibilities for curriculum resources. These units are given their mandate for teaching activity by the *Discipline* and, in this sense, act under the jurisdiction of the General Conference. Ordinarily, however, they function with considerable independence.

In most polities bishops play a critical role as "teachers" of the church, and a major understanding of a bishop's responsibility is his or her teaching office. This has not historically been the case in Methodism (with the possible theoretical exception of the bishops of the Methodist Episcopal Church, South). United Methodist bishops are spiritual leaders and conference managers.[3] They serve as executives in conference affairs. They possess influence of office and person, but since they have no vote in the General Conference, they do not directly participate in judgments about what the church should teach or do. They, in fact, execute the policies made by others. Even if functionally one can demonstrate that the bishops exercise greater power than they are explicitly granted, it remains the case that they cannot speak officially and authoritatively in regard to the authenticity of the apostolic message. The bishops have no directly delegated teaching function or office in The United Methodist Church.

There are two exceptions to these comments. First, the bishops must approve all liturgical changes. This role has been especially important in the approval of alternative services in United Methodism. Second, bishops do interpret the *Discipline*, and this is, as a matter of practice, a responsibility with teaching dimensions. *De facto* these two activities do recognize the role of the episcopacy in teaching.

There was a period—up until 1908—when the bishops in North American Methodism did possess a direct theological influence as they were empowered to approve all appointments to faculty positions in the church-related theological schools. The heresy trials of 1905–1908, however, made the bishops' role difficult, and their clear area of responsibility was surrendered. It is not an overstatement to say that bishops in The United Methodist Church currently play an insignificant role in speaking for the church in matters of theology, and a somewhat more important role, though still undefined, in guiding moral application. In the last reorganization of the Council of Bishops in 1976, one of the four committees was "Teaching Concerns," with a sub-committee on "Theological Education." This action gives evidence of the intention to exercise a greater influence on the teaching of the church.

The evolving character of the teaching office in the church may be seen in two recent actions. The first is evident in the bishops' pastoral *In Defense of Creation*. It is significant to note that this "pastoral" statement does not possess the same authority and power of a papal "pastoral." Instead, it embodies the advice of colleagueship and is, thereby, a contribution to conciliar discussion. This particular pastoral may prove to be an important initiative. Theological advice was sought, careful formulation was made, wide contribution was achieved, and much discussion has followed. This action may adumbrate an ongoing initiative by the Council of Bishops to lead theological reflection of the church; it may represent a claim for a teaching role. If so it represents a claim initiated by the bishops—rather than granted by the General Conference—and this may create a significant place for the bishops in the theological life of the church. Whether this will be remains to be seen.

The second action occurred in the 1972 and 1988 efforts to rewrite the theological section of the *Discipline*. In these actions the General Conference exercised its authority in the teaching office. This is a commendable and potentially important move—especially if it is not limited to one section of the *Discipline* or to an occasional activity of General Conferences.

The lack of clarity about the teaching office beyond or in addition to the official role of the General Conference has meant that functionally any responsibility for the exercise of this office devolves on each ordained minister. In the act of ordination, authority "to preach the word" is given, implying a teaching responsibility. Further, in the disciplinary statement of "Responsibilities and Duties of a Pastor" (paragraph 439) two possible references can be taken to refer to a teaching responsibility. Among the pastor's duties are the following:

a) To preach the Word, read and teach the Scriptures, and engage the people in study and witness. . . .
e) To instruct candidates for membership and receive them into the Church.[4]

The assumption in both cases seems to be that there is a clear and persisting understanding of the gospel, which pastors are to convey. The matter of assessing this proclamation is not addressed.

There are basic matters in this delegation of responsibility that need to be noted. First, a full teaching responsibility is not explicitly given, so the role must be interpreted from suggestions. Second, such a function tends toward individual interpretation and underplays the corporate responsibility of the church or of a congregation. Perhaps we should more clearly acknowledge the teaching responsibility of every ordained minister and seek ways both to establish corporate responsibility and to enable more consistent expression of this responsibility.

At the present time there is little explicit understanding of how the teaching office ought to be exercised. The General Conference has designated power, but little competence, sufficient time, or historically formed character to fulfill this task. Further, the Judicial Council does not function in such a manner as to engage theological issues; and the Council of Bishops has no directly delegated authority or history of activity that promises leadership in this area. Pastors do have some designated responsibility, but this function remains vague (perhaps because it assumes a clear understanding of the gospel).

Ambiguity about the teaching office extends to the role of persons who have teaching posts (such as professors in theological schools) that bear directly on the church's life and doctrine. Little guidance is given as to how they, in their teaching roles, relate to the ongoing life of the church or even to their ordination responsibilities. United Methodist churches have also not followed the example of those traditions (e.g., the Reformed) that practice ordination to a teaching role. Instead we continue to live with an unstable relationship between the general church and its theological schools and between persons with explicit teaching roles within the general life of the church and their ordination responsibilities.

Yet, I see possibilities: (1) for the bishops to be assertive and claim a central role, (2) for the General Conference and annual conferences to establish ongoing theological commissions, (3) for theological discussion to be a part of the General Conference's regular agenda (and derivatively, of Annual and District Conferences), and for clarification of the ''teaching office'' for pastors in local congregations, and (4) for rethinking the role of those whose vocation is teaching. Is it impossible to hope for these changes?

To pursue these possibilities I want to consider several issues that are important to an understanding of the teaching office in United Methodism: communal formation, teaching goals, and conciliarism and continuity.

Communal Formation

The nature of teaching itself must be examined. We teach not only when we explicitly intend to do so or when we attempt to instruct through stereotyped methods, but we also teach through those processes of community formation in the congregation— its life and rituals, its styles and concerns, its language and values. The church teaches by its common life, its worship, its mission, and its discipline. The church teaches through the context of its worship, hymnody, and prayers; by claims upon all community members to participate in the mission of God; and by mutual claims of community members upon one another. This total ethos is authoritative as it makes possible communal transmission of its distinctive life. A part of such teaching is specific reflection on doctrine and the community's way of life. Unfortunately, explicit theology has often been left aside in efforts at self-understanding in the church. The issue is how theology and the life of the church may be held together. Or can we be conscious of the multiple ways in which we instruct in our community, relate this to theological self-reflection, and reempower the formation of whole persons in mind as well as in heart and service?

For United Methodism, this inclusive mode of teaching is important, for it is in accordance with the role of theology within the life and faith of this tradition. The Wesleyan tradition is not primarily theological, but it is also theological, and this holism is a part of its distinctive character. Wesleyanism has stressed the wholeness of experience as thought, affection, will, and action. Wesleyan theology is found within the historical process of concrete Methodist bodies as they have worshiped and lived and taught, as they have developed institutions, assumed missional tasks, and found common symbols, rituals, and styles of life. As a part, and only as a part, of this total complex can Wesleyan theology be adequately appreciated.

These matters have implications for the teaching office in Methodism. That is, no isolated body of doctrine is to be taught as finally independent, neither the method of teaching (namely, clear recognition of the full range of communication) nor what is taught (namely, clear recognition that theology is part of a more complete and more adequate response of human beings to God). Theology is important, but not singular; the intellectual love of God is one aspect of a more inclusive love of God; teaching has to do not only with thoughts but also with the ways in which we live with one another in the world. The teaching office in Methodism, therefore, has a distinctive character and role. To teach is to contribute to the total formation of Christian life; teaching is done by deed and action as well as by word. And what is taught is not doctrine in an abstract way but "practical divinity"—that is, doctrine undergirding and enriching Christian existence.

Goals of Teaching

In traditional Methodist language, the goal of our teaching is the sanctification of persons and of congregations. To state the goal in this way is to move from an abstract intellectualism toward practical agency as persons in community with God and neighbors. Hence the goal of teaching in Methodism is not uniquely focused on rational consensus in doctrinal construction. The aim is holistic: We teach in order to provide authentic worship and service; teaching is for the sculpting of life. The means of teaching are totalistic: Teaching is a part of every activity and is effective as it conveys ways of living. Methodists

65

were not called people of method for no reason. The ordering of life in comprehensive terms was the shaping Christian response. Yet, we have tended to play down the importance of the methods of Methodists. One does not want to overstate what the methodical character of Methodism produced or portended, but this very means of formation points in the direction of a comprehensive sense of instruction and of the goals of teaching.

The goal of the sanctification of persons and of congregations informs the responsibility of teaching. That is, the teaching office is in the service of the achievement of these goals. So teaching is not singularly for intellectual maturation; rather teaching is for the transformation and enhancement of life as the worship of God and service to the neighbor. The office of teaching is that of a person or a community attempting to measure the ongoing life of the church by its source (namely, God in Christ through the Holy Spirit) and by the ongoing reign of God and its eschatological hope.

Perhaps this raises the question of the residence of authority in United Methodism. Authentic authority is conveyed by community and functions to organize or shape life according to the values of that community. Authority functions in a variety of modes and through numerous channels. Authority is accepted as valid when it nurtures life through means and toward goals that are acknowledged as possessing integrity, sensitivity, and value. The authorities that structure life for United Methodists are those received through the entire encompassing life of the local congregation and the ethos of the larger church. To be aware of what authorizes one's existence is important; covert authorities are pernicious, while overt authorities are not only recognized but may be challenged and utilized as well.

When we speak of authority we are not only asking who speaks for the church. We are asking how the church should speak authoritatively to its own life, in critique of its message

and in the ordering of life toward its goals. The problem is not
theoretical, but intensely practical. Theoretically we have seen
that the official authority in the church resides in the General
Conferences, but are not unofficial and less explicit authorities
also potent? Do not the regular worship service, the ongoing
tasks of mission, the disciplines of Christian formation, and the
sensibilities of a church community actually function authoritatively in our denomination's life? Obviously they do. Yet, all
of these modes of authorization need to be critically assessed;
they need to be judged against their normative source and the
continuing intention of God.

To look at the goals of teaching in The United Methodist
Church is to focus on what our teaching is for and,
consequently, to ask about our goals and about our effectiveness in achieving those goals. In a sense, every discussion of
policy or missional priority in a local church or General
Conference attempts this task. The point I am pressing is that
this should be done more regularly, formally, and intentionally.
Is an explicit group required for this task to be done well? Does
the General Conference need a theological commission?

Conciliarism and Continuity

Two issues found in a conciliar position require discussion.
First is the question: How may continuity be assured? This issue
is difficult because decisions are up for reconsideration every
time there is an official meeting. This is a problem for all
conciliar groups, and certainly for The United Methodist
Church, whose General Conference is self-organizing and
which, theoretically, may call everything into question except
what the restrictive rules prohibit. By which previous decisions
are we presently bound? Affirmation of the four ecumenical
creeds and the Articles on Religion are especially important in
answer to this question. But this affirmation is not always
recognized, and the question presses: Is there continuing

67

authoritative guidance? We are faced with the problem of how ongoing conciliar authority may be exercised. Can the authority of the General Conference be so utilized and accepted that it can function to fulfill the teaching office of the church?

Second, the concern for continuity raises a question regarding what body appropriately makes decisions for the church. Although General Conference membership involves some overlapping constituencies, it does not provide the certainty and continuity to be found in those churches with a strong and self-perpetuating hierarchy. There are also several levels of decision making at work in the church. Do local churches and annual conferences thereby have a legitimate role along with General Conference? To what extent is theological work exploratory and suggestive until it reaches the General Conference and is given (or not given) official status in the life of the church?

The type of decision being sought in conciliar meetings is also a critical matter. Doctrine is not being defined for all future time at every conciliar conference. While particular decisions explicitly relevant to contemporary issues may be enjoined, it is also appropriate for a teaching office to function by setting boundaries or by guiding the ways in which particular decisions should be made in the life of the church. The teaching of the church may include the development of conclusions, boundaries, or processes for discussion.

At this point, an ecumenical dimension to our discussion requires us to ask whether the appropriate body for teaching the church ultimately lies beyond denominational polities. Is the teaching of the General Conference itself to be shaped by participation in ecumenical bodies? What is the authority ascribed to such bodies as Faith and Order or the Lima Document on *Baptism, Eucharist and Ministry,* for instance? Obviously the authority of such activity for a conciliar body is as a contributor in the discussion. Is it more? At the present time it is not. But it is important to stress that ecumenical theological work makes a significant contribution to denominational teaching.

Conclusion

Any contemporary teaching office faces profound difficulties. Individualism, pluralism, and disregard for authority make teaching suspect and limited. A Faith and Order statement says boldly, "Today all concepts, ways and modes of teaching are being tested."[5]

Inherited modes of teaching are now questioned. We are challenged to be creative in imagining how teaching would be done in our time. We cannot teach authoritatively today by simply repeating the past. New times demand new responses.

In United Methodism we are especially in need of claiming the task of teaching at a variety of levels and by a variety of groups. Our conciliar tradition can continue to be the context of discussion, arguments, and recognition of new challenges. It can continue to be the form of our decision making about theological issues, and provide the context for future decisions about the shape and function of the teaching office of the church.

Since the responsibility of the teaching office has not been attended to in a conscious and thorough way, however, the following suggestions are made to facilitate this discussion in the church.

1. General Conference and Annual Conferences should make discussion of theology a regular and significant part of their agenda. These are the points at which conciliar decisions become a reality. To serve this purpose, conferences should appoint a permanent Theological Commission to which matters might be referred and that will have authority to study issues on its own. This commission should report regularly to the

General, Annual, and District Conferences, where its reports will be studied and acted upon.

2. The bishops of the church should continue to initiate study and make statements so as to provide leadership in the discussion of theological and ethical issues. In order to strengthen this role, paragraph 501 in the *Discipline* should be revised to include teaching as a part of the task of the bishops.

3. Local pastors should be directly encouraged to assume teaching responsibilities, and congregations should be encouraged to support this role.

4. There should be recognition of persons in church seminary teaching positions who could, along with their task, be specifically recognized in their appointment beyond the local church.

The establishment of a teaching office in The United Methodist Church that is consciously set and explicitly acknowledged would significantly serve the church. Such a responsibility would help to maintain the authenticity of the gospel we preach, it would provide more adequate bases for our ethical and missional activity, and it would make us critically aware of the values that underwrite the worship and order in the life of the church. Our church functions so as to teach in the totality of its communal life. It would be strengthened in its practice if what it teaches could be regularly and thoroughly assessed.

NOTES

1. See John C. Bowmen, *Pastor and People* (London: Epworth Press, 1975), pp. 121-25.

2. James Turner, in speaking of the revivalist tradition, comments,

"Their preachers became celebrated but not their professors" (*Without God, Without Creed* [Baltimore: The Johns Hopkins University Press, 1985], p. 75).

3. In the disciplinary description of the "Nature of Superintendency" (in paragraph 501), the responsibilities of a bishop are listed as ordering the life of the church, initiating structures and strategies for equipping Christian people for service, and administering matters temporal and spiritual. All of these tasks are gathered together under the rubric of "leadership." Both here and in listing the "Specific Responsibilities of Bishops" (paragraphs 514-16) no mention is made of a "teaching office" or any equivalent responsibility. Officially, therefore, bishops are not explicitly given this responsibility.

4. *The Book of Discipline of The United Methodist Church* (Nashville: The United Methodist Publishing House, 1988), p. 244.

5. "How Does the Church Teach Authoritatively Today?" *The Ecumenical Review* 31 (January 1979): 77.

III.
GUIDELINES FOR
CONTEMPORARY CONVERSATIONS
ON TEACHING

In the next two chapters, Robin Maas and Mary Elizabeth Mullins Moore shift the attention for our discussion from an exploration of past understandings to current denominational guidelines. Drawing upon *The Book of Discipline* and recent General Conference action, their chapters provide a critical perspective on our task. Maas challenges the church to reclaim a distinctive Methodist approach to scripture interpretation deeply rooted in its history. Moore challenges the church to attend to the distinctive way it approaches the task of doing theology. Questions that may focus your own thoughts about their discussion include the following:

1. What are the distinctive elements in a United Methodist approach to interpreting scripture and doing theology?

2. Where have you seen these elements guiding the teaching of the congregations you know, the educational decisions of the Annual Conference or general church agencies?

3. To what extent is it important to reclaim missing or diminished elements in United Methodist approaches to interpreting scripture or doing theology?

Chapter 4

Our Teaching Task:
Scripture in a Wesleyan Context

Robin Maas

The deliberations of the 1988 General Conference of The United Methodist Church were distinguished by the harmonious discussion and the ultimate adoption of a revised theological statement for the denomination. A critical portion of the statement—"Our Theological Task"—forcefully reasserts the primacy of Scripture as the chief source and criterion of doctrine and practice for United Methodists. It acknowledges, as well, the close interdependence between Scripture and three other sources and standards for doing theology: tradition, experience, and reason. While the revised document designates Scripture as the "living core" of Christian faith, it goes on to affirm that for United Methodists the Bible must be "illumined by tradition," "vivified by personal experience," and "confirmed by reason." Given the assignment to reflect on what is essential and normative in the teaching of Scripture in a Wesleyan context, it seems both appropriate and necessary to explore the distinctive interrelationship of Scripture, tradition, experience, and reason.

The Primacy of Scripture

The primacy of Scripture for Christians rests on the access it gives to the "living Christ [who] meets us in the experience of

77

redeeming grace.'' Because Scripture witnesses to the incarnate Word of God—Jesus of Nazareth—we grant it status and honor its own internal claims to ultimacy. The first—and last—consideration for the teaching church must always, then, be to bring people into direct, immediate contact with the Incarnate Word of God, Jesus, through the written word, Scripture.

Protestant Christianity has historically affirmed that the Bible alone contains all that is "necessary and sufficient unto salvation" (Articles of Religion), hence its primacy for faith and practice. Implicit in this historical assertion is an assumption that, up until the present century, seemed irrefutable. For many Christians, however, it has ceased to be operational or authoritative. I refer here to the conviction that the issues of salvation are, indeed, issues and that "salvation"—whatever it may mean—is something to be urgently desired and pursued with an uncompromising singleness of purpose. Specifically, I will argue that a truly existential acknowledgment of the authority of Scripture for faith and practice rests on a prior acknowledgment: that something genuinely momentous—namely, our eternal destiny—is at stake in the choice to become a follower of Jesus Christ.

A multitude of factors may combine to create that conviction in an individual. In the Wesleyan tradition, the net effect of such factors is identified with "prevenient grace," and because this conviction is a response to grace, it cannot be predicted or programmed. Nevertheless, at the very least, preaching and teaching that assume the primacy of Scripture must focus attention on the issues of salvation.

The common-sense concept of how to implement the primacy of Scripture in the church centers on the use of "biblically centered" curriculum resources designed to cover biblical content comprehensively. This is correct, as far as it goes. Most students entering seminary provide striking evidence of the

SCRIPTURE IN A WESLEYAN CONTEXT

failure of churches to develop a solid grasp of biblical information among their members. For the average first-year seminarian (a product of local church education), one of the great intellectual surprises and spiritual breakthroughs occurs through the discovery of the theological riches and complexity of the Bible in general and the Old Testament in particular.

At the very least, churches in the Wesleyan tradition must commit themselves to exposing their members to the *entire* biblical canon in a systematic, predictable way. Lectionary preaching moves the church significantly in this direction. Adult education programs based on comprehensive study series, such as *Genesis to Revelation* (Graded Press), are another hopeful sign. In contrast, the odd practice of publishing children's material containing made-up morality tales with fictional "biblical" characters is cause for continuing concern. Genuine biblical literacy is almost always a consequence of sustained study (usually at home) by the religiously committed individual. Numerous daily Bible study guides exist. The underlying issue, however, has to do with what convinces the individual Christian that he or she cannot live by bread alone—that the word of God is essential for life. Again, we are thrown back on the prior assumption that Scripture is not central until "everything" is at stake in whether or not we know the Incarnate Word of God. Most people know that they cannot get through the day without some form of material nourishment. The fact that so few are convinced that the bread of heaven is equally essential is not the fault of Scripture; it is a failure of preaching and teaching.

The Bible will not regain its central authority in the life of the church simply because United Methodists have decided to state—or restate—its primacy in an official or formal way. Actual or practical authority—which is the only kind that counts in Methodism—rests on the personal conviction of United Methodists, which, in turn, is a reflection of a broader ecclesial conviction. Surrounded today by a secular culture that has summarily dismissed traditional soteriological concerns, the church must somehow convince itself (once again) that "everything" ultimately hinges on its faithful witness to Jesus Christ, and that unless it self-consciously recovers and reemploys what I will call here a soteriological hermeneutic in the preaching and teaching of Scripture, it will be offering a stone in place of bread to people who are slowly but surely dying of starvation.

Illumined by Tradition

One of the things that never ceases to amaze me is the way in which the major denominations always seem to feel compelled to reinvent the wheel when it comes to teaching Scripture. This is most evident in the curriculum-publishing enterprise. Year in and year out, the churches keep printing new, improved Bible study materials and assorted curricula, and the local churches consume these curricula as children consume junk food. The consumption mentality in the production and use of printed curricula means, of course, that almost nothing is ever used twice.

Changing social, cultural, and political contexts do require fresh and relevant interpretations of Scripture, but printed curricula should not be relied on to provide that freshness and relevance. Since history does repeat itself in numerous ways, it is possible to find in the theological commentary of previous eras insights that are surprisingly relevant for today. John Wesley recognized this insight by compiling an impressively comprehensive library of (edited) Christian classics for his preachers and lay followers. Wesley's enormous spiritual hunger and eclectic proclivities led him to explore major areas of the tradition, not because they were arcane, but because they were "family history" so to speak; and since family history is essential to understanding who we are, it is always potentially relevant. What Wesley understood instinctively, and what the rest of us have been slow to grasp, is that the real issue in the use of traditional material is not relevance but accessibility.

The great virtue of printed curricula is that it is relatively cheap and easy to locate. Unfortunately, the riches of our common theological tradition are much less accessible. It would make good theological and economic sense for denominational publishing companies to begin to incorporate some carefully selected traditional material in their "new" curricula. The occasional scholarly biblical commentary will include material that shows how the church interpreted a given text in different eras. In theory, there is no reason why United Methodists, in the intellectually generous spirit of John Wesley, could not begin to produce Bible study materials that take into account what the church has had to say in previous generations about biblical themes and books. Available publications of books containing Wesley's sermons are very expensive. Why not produce curricula in which Wesley's sermonic treatment of particular biblical texts is laid side-by-side with a modern critically informed commentary? Material of this nature could result in surprising new insights about what is and is not relevant in the context of the contemporary believing community.

Obviously, more is at stake than simply informing people about what the church *used* to teach and preach. I have found in my own teaching of Scripture to laity (who hold widely divergent theological opinions) that no single resource serves better to defuse tensions over conflicting understandings of biblical authority than some basic information about the history of biblical interpretation. Simply to recognize that the battle between biblical literalists and non-literalists is not an exclusively modern, post-enlightenment phenomenon but has its ancient parallel in the Antiochian and Alexandrian schools of biblical interpretation is a profoundly liberating insight—and I don't mean just for the teacher! To witness the significantly different readings that Augustine, Luther, Calvin, and Wesley might all give the same biblical passage is to realize that no one really has the last word on the meaning of a text, but that throughout the ages great and faithful minds have found many ways to present the Word to people as sustaining bread.

This approach to the exposure of the history of biblical exegesis prevents—or at least curbs—the impulse to absolutize the culturally conditioned reading we, as twentieth-century North Americans, usually give a text. If the historical naivete of a previous epoch's exegetical method amuses or annoys us, we may be reminded that future generations will probably read our current efforts with the same degree of amusement or annoyance.

This discussion leads us to ask whether, in the choice of traditional material, any and all such traditions should be given equal time or weight. This is an important question for any denomination to ask. The amount of teaching time available in our churches is depressingly limited. We cannot afford to squander it by employing a smorgasbord approach to biblical education, even if we are historically conscious in our approach. To respond to this question, I would return to the issue of the prior concern for, and necessity of, a soteriological hermeneutic.

If all of Scripture must be studied in the light of what is at stake in becoming a disciple of Christ—in the light of the issues of salvation—then Wesleyan students of Scripture need to approach the Bible informed by what John Wesley taught about the issues of salvation. To be specific, United Methodists stand in a theological tradition that takes at least two soteriological doctrines with utmost seriousness. The first is justification, which Wesley identified with conversion and regeneration. The second is sanctification, which Wesley understood as a life-long process of "going on to Perfection." Both doctrines are biblical and both address themselves to defining with a good deal of precision what is at stake in the issues of salvation. This is particularly true in the case of the doctrine of Christian perfection, which Wesley inherited and then developed further in a direction that initially gave Methodism a unique (and controversial) soteriology. For United Methodism, these doctrines can be relied upon to help clarify some of the choices that face the teaching church about how to select biblical texts and traditional commentary as well as how to interpret this material in the light of pressing current affairs.

This solution sounds rational, but I do not think it will be particularly easy for United Methodists to implement, especially since most United Methodist pastors continue to be schooled in a scholarly tradition in which the hegemony of German Lutheran soteriological concerns remains for the most part unchallenged. (Interestingly, I would imagine that seminary students coming from the Reformed tradition, where the major soteriological doctrines are those of election and predestination would also be at a disadvantage, but perhaps less so.) We are naive if we ignore the soteriological biases of the authors of the textbooks we use in seminary for both biblical studies and systematic theology. The growing influence of social criticism in theological studies has clarified the inevitable lack of objectivity inherent in all theologizing. So be it. But no denomination concerned about the distinctiveness of its identity should passively allow itself to be gradually phased out of existence by a mindless eclecticism in theological content and method.

Vivified by Personal Experience

Having argued that for the teaching church to affirm the primacy of Scripture implies (minimally) faithful and systematic attention to (1) the entire biblical canon; and (2) the history of family involvement with these sacred documents—especially, in this case, the *Wesleyan* branch of the family—I come now to that area of concern that, historically, has most definitively characterized the people called Methodist: experience. The term *experience,* as used by John Wesley, referred specifically to religious experience, especially the converting, convicting experience of new birth. Nowadays the term is used much more loosely and often refers to social, cultural, and political realities in the lives of individual Christians. For example, in North American churches, ethnic minorities and women claim that the unique circumstances of their social condition necessarily impinge on the ways in which they experience God and the gospel. The Church Universal, likewise, is being forced to take account of compellingly different cultural contexts as these impinge on worship, catechesis, and mission. Cultural particularity is by no means a new phenomenon, but it is finally an officially recognized one, and the church is attempting to come to terms with it constructively as an enriching experience of diversity, and not simply as a threat to Christian unity.

In relation to the element of personal experience in the teaching of Scripture, at least three questions present themselves for our consideration. First, in the midst of so much cultural diversity, can the church look to any *common* or *core religious experience* as a basis for a unified vision of faith and practice? Second, given the radical diversity that exists among Christians, how can a culturally conditioned document such as the Bible claim primacy as either a basis of or criterion for evaluating religious experience? And third, what is the responsibility of the teaching church in relation to religious experience?

The answer to the first question is not hard to come by. From the earliest centuries the church has taught that a direct, personal encounter with the Risen Christ characterized by self-surrender is the basis for faithful discipleship. As Paul insisted, it is only in that personal and sacrificial encounter with Christ crucified that cultural, social, and gender differences are dissolved: "There is no longer Jew or Greek, there is no longer slave or free, there is no longer male and female; for all of you are one in Christ Jesus" (Gal. 3:28). In the very early church, that submission to the Incarnate Word of God was supported and sealed by the sacrament of baptism. Where infant baptism is practiced and children grow up never knowing themselves as other than Christian, then the issue of personal appropriation of the gospel becomes acute. Why? Because without that *common* experience of coming to know Christ in a direct and immediate way, without that moment of truth in which the claims of self are surrendered to the claims of perfect love, the unity of the church is necessarily threatened—for it is only *in Christ* that the differences are dissolved.

The experience of surrendering self to Christ can be counted on to contain certain common elements whether we be Jew or Greek, male or female. It is an immensely humbling, relativizing experience, bringing both pain and joy in its wake. It is the assuming of a yoke, a burden that is—ironically, amazingly—liberating. It is something the converted—usually after years of evasion—finally run to embrace.

The family history, gathered from every part of the globe, testifies abundantly and persuasively to these common features of what it means to put on Christ, and so, of course does Scripture. This brings us to the second question: How can we reconcile ecclesial claims of scriptural primacy with a document that is so obviously culturally conditioned itself? To answer that, we have to go back to the soteriological question.

It is always a little embarrassing for the Christian to have to witness to a Messiah, a Savior, who was himself culturally conditioned. It is intellectually difficult to assert that at a particular moment in time the sovereign transcendent God of Israel chose to assume human nature in the form of a carpenter rabbi from Nazareth whose fate was to end up with a criminal conviction and a public execution. No one in her or his right mind would dream up a salvation scenario like this one! Theologians call this the scandal of particularity; but whatever we call it, it is a hard gospel to preach, a difficult mouthful to swallow. That the Bible should recount this amazing story not only without embarrassment but also triumphantly (even gloatingly!) should certainly give us pause. But at least it clarifies the choice. It tells us clearly what is at stake.

Given the reality of what God did, it seems inevitable that Scripture's witness to this act of divine folly and our witness, too, must be culturally conditioned. There is no way to avoid this conclusion. *God's* choice condemns us to the particular; and this means that we will not find Truth beyond the limitations of our creatureliness but in and through this creatureliness. So, too, with the Bible. The truth of Scripture, the very basis for its authority, is in its manifestation of a particular—that is, an embodied—saving relationship between the Creator of all that is and a tiny, obscure, and obstreperous people. Strangest of all is the biblical claim that each one of us has been invited into that same relationship by means of a single Person (not a Principle) chosen by Yahweh to be a "light to the Gentiles." Yet, it is on this strange claim that any ecclesial claim for scriptural primacy must ultimately rest.

The third question is the toughest and most embarrassing of all: If the practical primacy of Scripture rests on its own internal witness to a life-giving relationship with Jesus Christ, then what does this say about the responsibility of the teaching church? There is a widespread, naively optimistic notion everywhere in the mainstream churches that if we just expose people to the Bible as the "Word of God" they will naturally want to accept its teachings and live by them. This is particularly evident in our Sunday school and catechetical programs, where little if anything is done to disabuse parents of the notion that the main reason for educating a child in the faith is to make a "good person" out of him or her.

I suppose that if the churches and Sunday schools actually succeeded in making "good persons" out of all attendees we would be justified in considering them successful beyond our wildest dreams. But this is not what our enterprise is supposed to be about, and here again I am relying on a particular vision of salvation that is true to the teaching and preaching of John Wesley, who was himself true to the longer tradition of Christian orthodoxy. The goal of the Christian life in the Wesleyan theological tradition is not simply a forgiven sinner or even a "good," morally upright person. The goal for each individual Christian is nothing less than *holiness.*

Holiness is a word in serious need of creative rehabilitation in United Methodism, and although the limitations of this chapter preclude an adequate exposition of what Wesley intended when he made use of this word, we can affirm that the point of holiness was the consummation of this very same relationship with Christ that has occupied our attention thus far. The act of union requires an essential likeness between whatever or whomever is to be united. Just as the good tree brings forth good fruit and not bad, so also holiness begets more holiness. To commence a relationship with Christ—to "put on" Christ, to be grafted onto the true Vine—is *to place ourselves in a position to be sanctified*—to begin that long journey toward perfect love of God and neighbor.

Unfortunately, this will not just happen. Although we occasionally hear of a dramatic conversion that occurs because someone has been given a Bible to read, this is usually not the type of situation most of us face in the local church. Just as we do not expect to teach mathematics by handing a textbook to someone and saying, "Go thou and compute," so also we should not expect to bring a person into a saving relationship with Christ simply by exposing her or him to the Bible.

A good teacher, faced with introducing the student to a new idea, a new reality, will take the student by the hand (metaphorically speaking) and lead, at the proper pace, him or her through a series of steps until the process has been mastered. In the first place, the teacher models competence; this skill is important and worth mastering. In the second place, the teacher embodies empathy and compassion, being quick to anticipate obstacles, patient but firm in the face of indifference or resistance, rejoicing over each little victory on the road to mastery. It is almost always the teacher, and not the textbook, who brings the student to a new level of competence. The teacher does so by means of the textbook, which is indispensable as both a teaching and a learning tool. Eventually the student will use the book without the teacher's assistance, but it is *the teacher's* enthusiasm and *the teacher's* mastery of the subject matter that makes the whole proposition a likely matter for consideration.

By and large the teaching church has not succeeded in helping people encounter Jesus Christ in a personal and immediate way. Some may say this statement sounds too much like evangelism. But in the church the pedagogical task *does* have an evangelical dimension. It must if the church is to be anything other than a holding operation. Specifically, where the church has failed most significantly in its teaching of Scripture is in the matter of the *devotional* use of Scripture. The scriptures provide not only the incentive but also the means to enter into a saving relationship with God through Christ. They teach us how to pray; they give us material with which to pray. The four Gospel portraits of Jesus of Nazareth give us our first and most effective introduction to the human face of God. Even so, the teacher who does not pray the scriptures will not be able to teach others to do so with any kind of conviction or persuasiveness.

Judging from most of the curricula I have seen, the issue of personal appropriation gets taken care of by means of discussion questions, such as "What does this mean to you (or us) today?" There is nothing wrong with asking this kind of question, but its vagueness permits—perhaps encourages—evasiveness. Much of the time, an honest answer would be "I don't know," and it is here that so much teaching fails. More pointed questions—"What kind of claims does this passage make for Jesus Christ?"; "What kind of claims does it make on you?"; "Where do you find yourself responding positively to these claims?"; "Where are the points of personal resistance?"; "What is at stake for you in how you respond to these claims?"—would probably help. But there is a terrible timidity—almost a conspiracy of silence—among teachers at every level, from the seminary to the Sunday school, about the whole business of prayer and its relationship to the issues of salvation. This timidity gives the lie to every self-confident and self-righteous attack we make on individualism and privatism in matters of faith. We, who hold such public positions of trust in the life of the church, have kept our religious experience and our devotional life to ourselves, and the church is now paying a steep price for our reticence.

Confirmed by Reason

It is with respect to the last of these four sources and standards that the mainstream churches, including The United Methodist Church, have been most successful in achieving some kind of consensus about how to deal with Scripture. The denomination as a whole and its seminaries in particular have embraced both the insights and the ethos of historical-critical biblical scholarship and, in recent years especially, attempted to produce preaching and teaching materials that honor the biblical commandment to love God with all our mind. In this, United Methodism has tried to follow the spirit of its founder even if it has not always succeeded in emulating his intellectual rigor in approaching the task. Yet, even here, countervailing cultural forces make a common pedagogical strategy and concerted action difficult.

Despite Wesley's enthusiastic endorsement of the critical scholarship of his day, contemporary United Methodists often perceive the application of critical reason to the biblical material as threatening to faith, and this is just as true in seminaries as it is in the local church—perhaps even more so. Part of this intellectual insecurity may be due to a superficial acquaintance with the Bible; most of it is a consequence of the lack of a healthy, vigorous devotional life in which Scripture has played a formative and sustained role. If, as a consequence of an encounter with Scripture, a Christian has felt the real presence of God in his or her life, he or she will not find faith destroyed—sorely tested perhaps, but not destroyed—by a later encounter with Norman Perrin or Rudolph Bultmann. And, if I am correct in this assumption, then it simply underscores the essential truth of the claim that reason and experience are necessarily interdependent in the life of faith.

The kind of training our seminarians receive assumes the value of historical-critical biblical research, so much so that many of our students complain that what we are teaching them is not Scripture, but historical-critical method. If this is the case, the real problem may not be that we teach too much historical-critical method, but, rather, that we teach too little. (A little learning, you will recall, can be a dangerous thing!) The demands of most seminary curricula, which reflect the job description of the typical pastor, normally do not permit much more than the briefest and most perfunctory exposure to either the content of Scripture or to exegetical technique. If students then arrive at seminary without having had a sustained exposure to Scripture, all the ingredients for a major pedagogical (not to mention religious) problem are in place. Since many graduates leave seminary unprepared academically and psychologically to apply their God-given reason to the study of Scripture in a disciplined, fruitful way, it follows that they will be equally ill-equipped to teach others to do the same.

Conclusions

It seems self-evident, then, that a truly Wesleyan approach to the teaching of Scripture must include (1) a systematic approach to biblical content in which the entire canon becomes the focus of attention; (2) the cultivation of a longer ecclesial memory, so that each succeeding generation stands to benefit from the practical religious wisdom of previous generations in the task of interpreting Scripture; (3) intentional guidance in and support for the devotional use of Scripture to the end that each individual may encounter Jesus Christ in a personal, immediate way; and (4) sustained attention to the task of equipping both clergy and laity with a set of critical study skills and the open, inquiring, and disciplined habits of mind needed to practice these skills with persistence and integrity.

Finally, none of these efforts will function effectively in isolation from one another and without some kind of governing soteriological perspective or hermeneutic to order them. For a denomination in the Wesleyan tradition, such a perspective must have obvious *practical* significance. It must be seen to make a real difference in the way people actually live out their faith. The vision that fired John Wesley was a vision of holiness—the perfect love of God and neighbor that our Lord identified as the essential prerequisite to union with God. For Wesley, nothing could have more immediate and practical consequence for Christian faith and practice than the quest for holiness of heart and life. If that vision no longer fires the imagination of United Methodists, then what will?

Chapter 5

Our Teaching Task:
Doing Theology

Mary Elizabeth Mullins Moore

Any attempt to take the pulse of the large and complex theological tradition of The United Methodist Church may be considered presumptuous. The effort, however, helps to name who we are and reflect on who we want to be. In this chapter we will undertake that effort by describing the character and dynamics of United Methodist theology and by drawing some conclusions about the teaching office within the denomination.

The pulse-taking will make use of four approaches because the task is so complex. Attention will be given to United Methodist practices of theological reflection, marks of United Methodist theology, recent theological developments, and shifts in theological perspective within the denomination. Teaching implications will be drawn both from the practice and the common themes within the United Methodist theological tradition. The conclusions for the teaching office are rich, especially regarding approaches, content, and structures for teaching.

United Methodist Practices of Theological Reflection
How do United Methodists do theology? Our denomination's style is a little like riding a mule down into the Grand Canyon. A

few years ago, my daughter and I made our first mule journey into the canyon, fulfilling a dream I had held for more than twenty years. Our situation looked something like this: My mule walked just two inches from the edge of the steep trail, overlooking an even steeper drop-off. We had a guide in front of us, but he was far away. We also had a guide at the end of the line, but he was taking a new mule down for the first time. Before we reached our destination, this guide's mule charged the other mules four times. When we finally reached the level land below, it threw the guide onto a prickly pear cactus and ran away. The guide stood up, trembling visibly. He finally rounded up the wandering mule and begged the more seasoned guide to trade mules. The seasoned guide insisted that the wary young man stay with his nervous mule because it would be good for both of them.

In the meantime, I was making friends with Frog (my jumping mule) and with the other people in the group. I was pondering the vastness of God's world, the indescribable beauty of the moment, my own fears, and the craziness of sending this new mule down with greenhorns like us. I felt daring and grateful to be so close to the wonders of millions of years and the awesome movements that had made the Grand Canyon.

This is the way that United Methodists do theology—on the run! United Methodists dream of ideas that would be good for the church—ideas for action or belief or structure. The denomination then seeks to put the ideas into practice, often over a period of time and with some false starts. Often the efforts are not effective because they are begun too late to win the church's support and get the vote. Sometimes the efforts are intensified and rushed when the conditions seem right and leaders are convinced there is no time to lose.

With the implementation of these new ideas, the church may begin to think about what it has done, sometimes wondering,

"Whose idea was this anyway?" But, by that time, it is too late to turn back. Church folk find themselves involved in a movement or cause or program that leads them down the edge of a steep path with an even steeper drop-off. The guide (if there is one) seems far away, and the guide at the rear of the line is taking a new mule down for the first time. This person is no help as a guide, and furthermore, has no idea how to deal with the new movement. The rear guide actually threatens everyone because he or she keeps charging ahead and starting an avalanche of uncontrolled movement. This frightens everyone, even allowing the movement to run away at times.

In the meantime, these United Methodist folk make friends with one another as they journey; they ponder the vastness of God's world, the indescribable beauty of the moment, their own fears, and the craziness of this new movement. They feel daring and grateful to be so close to the wonders of life and the historical movements that have led them to this place.

The metaphor of mule riding calls attention to certain features in the United Methodist practices of theological reflection. First, theology is continually being done. It usually takes place while the church is moving, rather than as a precondition to denominational action. The 1972 doctrinal statement, for example, was written as an outgrowth of the 1968 merger between the former Methodist and Evangelical United Brethren Churches. More recently, the 1976 decision by the General Conference to introduce diaconal ministry into the church's ministerial structures had led to four theological study commissions on the ministry (one each quadrennium) and the expansion of the section on the theology of ministry in *The Book of Discipline* in every subsequent quadrennium.

United Methodist theological practice is sometimes motivated by wonder, sometimes by fear, and sometimes by the need to analyze the craziness of the present situation. The 1984 General Conference, for example, mandated the Council of Bishops to appoint a committee to write a new theological statement to be presented at the 1988 General Conference. The motivation behind this action encompassed a mixture of wonder-filled hope that The United Methodist Church would give serious attention to its theology, fear of the pluralism that so characterized the denomination, and a need to analyze and sort out the variety of theological currents running through the denomination.

Moments of celebration compose a third feature of the United Methodist approach to theological reflection. They occur when people stop to express gratitude for living on the cutting edge, dare to walk down the precipice, and move close to the wonders of life. Celebration marked the response of delegates returning from the General Conference, pleased that the theological and mission statements adopted satisfied everyone on some points. One pastor, who had supported the Houston Declaration and its attempt to preserve certain traditional doctrines and language, wrote to his parishioners, saying that they would be pleased to know that conservative Christian principles had not been compromised in the new statements. Another pastor, an open critic of the Houston Declaration, told his parishioners that the discussions and revisions of the statements were open and conciliatory and the statements were good; he was proud of them. Celebration was shared by each, not only for the statements, but also for the conciliar process that led to their adoption.

Marks of United Methodist Theology

What kind of theological interpretations emerge out of the theological practices described above? Although the metaphor of the mule ride may be playful, the processes it helped us describe above distinguish certain marks in United Methodist theology that continually appear as theological reflection takes place quadrennium after quadrennium. These marks describe the United Methodist theological enterprise rather than establishing a list of common doctrines and beliefs. (More will be said about belief later.) These marks include, but are not restricted to, practicality, discipline, fluidity and constancy, connection, breadth, and universal-mindedness.

To begin, United Methodist theology is *practical*. The mark of practicality has been an enduring part of the style of United Methodist theology. The 1988 General Conference adopted a new Paragraph 66 for *The Book of Discipline,* entitled "Our Doctrinal Heritage," which makes this point. The prologue to a discussion of characteristic doctrines in the tradition traces this mark back to John Wesley: "The underlying energy of the Wesley theological heritage stems from an emphasis upon practical divinity, the implementation of genuine Christianity in the lives of believers."[1] The characteristic Wesleyan doctrines actually grew from these concerns for practical divinity, for Wesley "considered doctrinal matters primarily in terms of their significance for Christian discipleship."[2] Both the life of the individual Christian and the organization of the church affected theological formulations, and these formulations in turn influenced Christian living and church polity. The relationship was interactive.

A second mark of United Methodist theology is *discipline.* Theology is done in a disciplined manner and for the sake of discipline; in other words, the church engages in theological reflection for the sake of ordering life toward the fullness of salvation. The discipline includes an organization for doing theology. In eighteenth-century Britain the Methodist societies and similar societies in the United Brethren Church and Evangelical Association emphasized edifying believers and spreading scriptural holiness. Discipline continues to be observable in the church today, with local churches, annual conferences, and general boards and agencies clearly organized and mandated to foster theological proclamation and teaching.

The work of the church itself is defined as taking place under the discipline of the Holy Spirit. The Preamble of the Constitution of The United Methodist Church states: "Under the discipline of the Holy Spirit the Church seeks to provide for the maintenance of worship, the edification of believers, and the redemption of the world."[3] The importance of discipline may be seen in the *Discipline,* which provides the theological and organizational framework for the church. The mark of discipline, in other words, encompasses the organizational structures of the church, the guidance from the Holy Spirit, and the church's *discipline* for the whole theological enterprise.

The third mark of United Methodist theology is *fluidity and constancy.* The degree of fluidity and constancy in all formal theological discussions has been widely debated in the denomination, including those that produced the 1988 "Doctrinal Standards and Our Theological Task." This theme harkens back to John Wesley's own approach to theological reflection. Wesley read and reproduced historical treatises widely, but also critiqued and offered alternatives to historical positions. He maintained the Anglican Articles of Religion for his movement, but also made some changes and selections from them.

The United Methodist Church has frequently debated the issue of fluidity and constancy in relation to the first Restrictive Rule in the Constitution: "The General Conference shall not revoke, alter, or change our Articles of Religion or establish any new standards or rules of doctrine contrary to our present existing and established standards of doctrine."[4] This rule led to considerable discussion as to whether the Confession of Faith of the Evangelical United Brethren could be placed side by side with the Methodist Articles of Religion after the merger in 1968. The theological statement finally adopted by the denomination in 1972 not only included both doctrinal statements (constancy), but also spoke forthrightly about the desire of the denomination to avoid giving final authority to any doctrinal statement (fluidity). The interplay of constancy and fluidity may also be seen in the 1972 document, which states that the first two Restrictive Rules are not to be interpreted literally, but the people are encouraged to make "free inquiry within the boundaries defined by four main sources and guidelines for Christian theology: Scripture, tradition, experience, reason."[5] Fluidity and constancy have been a source of contention as well as a clear mark of the United Methodist style of theology.

A fourth mark of United Methodist theology is *connection.* The emphasis on connection goes back to the early roots of the Methodist movement. John Wesley established circuits for the sake of itinerating preachers and implementing ministry across all of the churches; he established societies, classes, and bands as interdependent structures for inspiration, nurture, and accountability.

The theological work in the early Methodist movement took place in the connection, primarily in the Conference. The minutes of early Wesleyan Conferences are filled with theological discourse, especially Wesley's presentation of answers to frequently asked questions. After the time of Wesley, the theological discourse continued in Conference and connectional settings, but without the reliance on one central person.

This process of communal theologizing within the connection has been referred to as a conciliar process. In the 1972 theological statement, the pioneers of the United Methodist traditions are described as operating by a conciliar, rather than a confessional, principle. Thus they did not function from a "claim that the essence of Christian truth can, and ought to be, stated in precisely defined propositions, legally enforceable by ecclesiastical authority."[6] Instead these early leaders "turned to a unique version of the ancient 'conciliar principle,' in which the collective wisdom of living Christian pastors, teachers, and people was relied upon to guard and guide their ongoing communal life.''[7]

Given the denomination's past, the continuation of the conciliar process seems appropriate, and references to the communal process do indeed carry over into the 1988 theological statement. It affirms that "our theological task is communal," and includes all United Methodist constituencies, every congregation, laity and clergy, bishops, boards, agencies and theological schools.[8] In practice, the General Conference sponsors and adopts the doctrinal guidelines for the connection. Doctrinal disputes are referred to Annual and General Conferences. Although the status and function of doctrinal standards continues to be somewhat ambiguous, the 1972 theological statement refers "otherwise irreconcilable doctrinal disputes" to "the Annual and General Conferences" as "the appropriate courts of appeal, under the guidance of the first two Restrictive Rules (which is to say, the Articles and Confession, the *Sermons* and the *Notes*).''[9]

These various conciliar practices are described in chapter 3 of this book, "Teaching in the Methodist Tradition" by Thomas A. Langford (pages 57-71). He identifies several complications that have emerged in the process, particularly from the ambiguity regarding the teaching office of pastors and bishops. Whatever the strengths and the complications, however, doing theology has been a connectional concern in The United Methodist Church.

A fifth mark of United Methodist theological discourse is *breadth*. The theological reflections of the church have been far-reaching and inclusive of many different kinds of concerns. Considerable attention has been given to theological method by the denomination; this emphasis is represented most vividly in the 1972 and 1988 theological statements, in which the guidelines (1972) or criteria (1988) for theological reflection (Scripture, tradition, experience, and reason) are put forth.[10]

Other concerns often expressed in theological reflections have included historical doctrines, rules for disciplined living, and principles for social responsibility.

A final mark of United Methodist theology will be mentioned here, though this list is by no means exhaustive. The denomination's theological reflections have been *universally minded*. Again, John Wesley set the example. He wanted to spread scriptural holiness as broadly as possible, stating at one point that "the world is my parish." He drew upon resources from the larger Christian tradition, including Orthodox, Roman Catholic, Moravian and other sources from his Anglican and pietistic British background. His eloquent speaking and writing on the concerns of British miners and on slavery in Britain and other parts of the world reveal his awareness of the broad social context and social mission of the church. He encouraged the unity of the church to be preserved wherever possible. His insistence in keeping the early Methodist movement within the Anglican Church may be the most profound example of his concern for unity. This universal orientation continues to be evident in the life and documents of The United Methodist Church. The Preamble of the Constitution includes these words: "The Church of Jesus Christ exists in and for the world, and its very dividedness is a hindrance to its mission in that world."[11] The mission statement adopted by the 1988 General Conference and the Social Principles, which have been part of *The Book of Discipline* in some form since 1908, reiterate the church's concern for the whole world and its desire to work in cooperation with other Christian bodies everywhere. The theological statements of 1972 and 1988 affirm the richness of the whole Christian tradition and the importance of the whole tradition to the theological task of The United Methodist Church. Similarly, both affirm the theological contributions that come from various cultures and communities around the globe. The denomination has been more ambiguous about relating with other religious traditions, but both of the recent theological statements call for explorations that may lead to more mutual understandings.

This introduction to the practices and marks of United Methodist theology establishes the background for analyzing the most recent theological movements in the denomination and identifying the challenges that lie ahead for the teaching office of the church. It is to those tasks that we next turn our attention.

Formation of New Theological Statements 1988

Lively theological discussions have characterized the 1980s. The 1984 General Conference recommended three new study commissions for The United Methodist Church. Two will be discussed here. One was to prepare a revision of the 1972 theological statement, and the other was to create a new statement on the mission of the church. Both commissions, along with the other commission to study the ministry, were to be appointed by the Council of Bishops, and both were to offer guidance to the church. The membership of the commissions included laity and clergy, theological scholars and bishops, men and women, and persons of different ethnic communities. The bishops expressed some concerns to both commissions, and the theological commission was asked to consider the problems of pluralism and doctrinal identity for the denomination.

The two commissions on theology and mission recognized early in their work the need to communicate with each other, so they had one formal meeting during the quadrennium and several informal consultations. The theological commission also made an early decision to revise the 1972 theological statement rather than to write an entirely new statement.

The work of these two commissions took place within the larger ecumenical discussions on theology and mission. The Faith and Order Commission of the World Council of Churches has been working to define and describe apostolic faith, a term that has found its way into the United Methodist theological statement. The Faith and Order Commission has centered its work on the Nicene-Constantinopolitan Creed, a summary of apostolic faith, representing the last official creed of the church before it divided between East and West. The Faith and Order Commission has offered the Creed as a test of the faith expressions of later Christian bodies, making clear that the quest for theological norms from the early church may be found in the theological constructions of ecumenical bodies and the United Methodist commissions.

A further contextual note should be made. The United Methodist Church encompasses considerable theological diversity, which is articulated in forthright and politically active terms. Several groups have formed to express their theological convictions and influence the directions of the church. Some, like Good News, have organized as ongoing groups. Others gathered primarily to produce documents for the consideration of the 1988 General Conference including the "Houston Declaration," "Chicago Declaration," and "Perfect Love Casts Out Fear." Although outside the formal organizational structures for theological reflection, these social dynamics within the church undoubtedly influenced the shape of the theological document that was produced, revised, and finally adopted by the General Conference.

The earliest drafts of the theological and mission statements produced by the commissions were not discussed widely in the general church, and no mechanism for broad-based discussion was implemented. The drafts did undergo considerable discussion and revision within the commissions themselves, in dialogue with the Council of Bishops, and in a joint meeting of the commissions. Later drafts were also discussed in the Oxford Institute of Methodist Studies, by several leaders of general boards and agencies, and among theological school faculties.

Many suggestions were addressed to the two commissions informally, and considerable debate took place regarding the statements in *Circuit Rider* and *The Christian Century*. Both commissions took these responses very seriously and did revisions until the final deadlines.

Then, the documents were circulated to General Conference delegates, who began to discuss them in their respective delegations. These discussions contributed to further revisions by the legislative committee on Faith and Mission during the General Conference deliberations. Thomas A. Langford, who chaired the legislative committee and was a prime drafter of the mission statement, encouraged the legislative committee to "model how we do theology." The collegial and frank process of the committee contributed to a growing consensus for the document that was finally presented to the General Conference, where it received 94 percent concurrence.[12]

The two documents underwent considerable revision from the first to the last drafts. Substantive revisions were made, including a reordering of the sources of authority so that Scripture was not set apart from tradition, experience, and reason; a greater emphasis on the interaction among the four sources and the possibility that theological reflection may begin in any of the four; a modification of normative language; an expansion of the meanings of experience and reason to include the breadth of human experience and reason and not simply experiencing and reasoning about the biblical witness; and an expanded statement of the church's ecumenical and interfaith commitments. Such revisions obviated some of the sharp differences between the 1972 and 1988 theological statements without obliterating them. The revisions reflected a dynamic process of dialogue in the denomination, not necessarily preplanned to continue the communal and conciliar processes described above, but certainly reflecting the fact that those processes continue to be alive and vital.

In addition to adopting the theological statement and commending the missional statement for study in the churches, General Conference made Faith and Mission a standing committee of the Conference. They also adopted a theme for the next quadrennium that reflects the central theme of the mission statement: "Celebrate and Witness," or "Celebrate God's Grace: Witness for Jesus Christ."[13] Both moves were intended to keep theology and mission in the forefront of the church.

Theological Shifts from 1972 to 1988

What theological shifts are represented by these recent developments? A comparative study of the two theological statements of 1972 and 1988 reveals many continuities, some of which have been described earlier in the discussion of the marks of United Methodist theology. The continuities are considerably greater with the final version of the 1988 document than with earlier versions. In fact, some language from the 1972 statement was reintroduced into the new statement. In this section of the chapter, however, my focus will be on the shifts made in the new statement. Eight shifts will be identified and briefly described. Again, this list is not exhaustive, but it points to trends that are potentially the most influential shifts.

The first and most profound shift in the 1988 theological statement is the move to be more normative in the approach to doctrine. This shift probably gives rise to many of the other shifts and has particularly strong influence on the teaching office of the church, so it will be developed at greater length. The shift toward doctrinal normativity is reflected in the new title of Part II of the *Discipline*. "Doctrine and Doctrinal Statements and the General Rules" has been replaced by "Doctrinal Standards and Our Theological Task." The language of standards, criteria, and validity in the new theological statement replaces the language of guidelines. The more open acknowledgment of diverse points of view replaces

105

the emphasis upon the dynamic of critique within the Christian tradition itself.

One example of this shift is evident in the new statement's introduction to the heritage that United Methodists share with Christians of all times and places: "This heritage is grounded in the apostolic witness to Jesus Christ as Savior and Lord, which is the source and measure of all valid Christian teaching.''[14] The earlier statement read: "There is a core of doctrine which informs in greater or less degree our widely divergent interpretations. From our response in faith to the wondrous mystery of God's love in Jesus Christ as recorded in Scripture, all valid Christian doctrine is born. This is the touchstone by which all Christian teaching may be tested.''[15] This is one of the few places where the word *valid* is used in the earlier statement, and it refers back to "our response in faith,'' leaving room for divergent interpretations and appealing to scriptural and doctrinal guidelines for testing interpretations. The new statement not only eliminates the rejoinder about different interpretations, but also refers to the apostolic witness as "the source and measure of all valid Christian teaching.''

This, of course, is only one example of the shift toward a normative status of doctrine, and it is subtle. Several other examples may be summarized briefly: (1) the removal of language recognizing and affirming pluralism (the word *pluralism* is not used at all in the new document, and the word *diversity* is used sparingly);[16] (2) the description of Scripture as the primary source and criterion for doctrine, rather than the primary source and guideline;[17] and (3) a more normative interpretation of the work of our theological forebears and the history of doctrinal authority. The first two sections are now entitled "Our Doctrinal Heritage'' and "Our Doctrinal History.'' They detail the status of doctrine in the church at large as well as in the pioneers of The United Methodist Church. The earlier statement focused, instead, on the way our forebears followed a conciliar principle more than a confessional principle. The earlier statement consequently gave far less attention to the status of doctrine in general.[18]

The degree of this shift to normativity can be overemphasized because the new statement, in its final version, does have some recognition of diversity and of the critical and communal nature of the theological enterprise discussed earlier. In fact, the theological task is described in one section as being critical, constructive, conciliar, and a matter of individual responsibility, reminding the reader that the Christian truth is not a complete and unequivocal given. The new emphasis, however, is decidedly different, and the differences are expressed in the structure, thematic emphases, and language of the two theological statements. In short, the two statements seem to have been written to answer very different questions. In the earlier statement, the dominant question seems to be: "How do we do theology faithfully in the context of a rich tradition and a pluralistic church and world?" In the later statement, the dominant question seems to be: "How do we do theology that clearly defines our Christian identity in relationship to our doctrinal tradition and offers standards for judging the adequacy of theological formulations?"

The second shift in the new theological statement is an appeal to history for answers to questions of faith. The expansion of the historical material provides vivid evidence of this trend. The frequent appeal to the Wesleyan heritage as the rationale for a particular belief or practice reinforces the shift. One example may be found in the description of experience: "In our theological task, we follow Wesley's practice of examining experience, both individual and corporate, for confirmations of the realities of God's grace attested in Scripture."[19] The frequent appeals to Wesley and other forebears are somewhat ironic in that more weight is being placed on tradition (even appealing to it as a starting point) than the description of tradition in the statement would warrant.

A third shift relates to the first two—namely, that the appeal to theological method moves from a more critical and constructive theology to a more applied theology. Both the normative status given to doctrine and the dominant appeal to history for answers to questions of faith suggest a theological method that is less critical of the tradition itself, less constructive in response to new revelation, and less open to new interpretations in the light of faith experience in the contemporary world. Appeals to the conciliar principle, flexibility, doctrinal development, loyalty and freedom, pilgrim people, and non-literalism have been removed from the earlier statement.[20] At this point both fluidity and mystery have been deemphasized.

Again, the differences are subtle, but real. For example, the new statement does reveal a fluid perspective on the Wesleyan tradition: "The heart of our task is to reclaim and renew the distinctive United Methodist doctrinal heritage."[21] The statement also has a fluid perspective on the theological task: "Our theological task includes the testing, renewal, elaboration, and application of our doctrinal perspective in carrying out our calling 'to spread scriptural holiness over these lands.' "[22] Such statements do not call for theological rigidity, but differ from the references in the 1972 statements to the historical contexting of doctrinal statements, the attempt "to appropriate the contributions of our Christian past even as we also stretch forward toward the Christian future," the "pressing need of renewed effort both to repossess our legacy from the churches we have been and to re-mint this for the church we aspire to be."[23]

The shift in theological method is also evident in the renewed emphasis on applied approaches to theology and ethics. "The General Rules and Christian Social Concerns" has been removed from the historical background material. The history of doctrine has been elaborated, while the history of practice has been deemphasized. The relationship between theology and ethics, consequently, is less emphasized, and the role of ethical practices in giving rise to theological beliefs is not considered. Instead, attention is given to the application of theology to Christian living, which is an applied appropriation of theology to ethics.[24]

A fourth change in the 1988 document is closely connected to the different perspectives on theological method. This is the shift in the approach to Scripture in relation to tradition, experience, and reason. Both documents affirm the primacy of Scripture, but the relationship between Scripture and the other sources is shifted in the new document. In earlier drafts of the 1988 document, a complete organizational and descriptive separation of Scripture was offered. This is greatly modified in the final 1988 document, but the Bible is still separated from tradition, experience, and reason in much of the language. One example is found in the description of Scripture in relation to the rest of the quadrilateral: "The Wesleyan heritage . . . directs us to a self-conscious use of these three sources in interpreting Scripture and in formulating faith statements based on the biblical witness."[25] Another example is the tendency to relativize tradition, but not Scripture: "But the history of Christianity includes a mixture of ignorance, misguided zeal, and sin. Scripture remains the norm by which all traditions are judged."[26] Such statements about Scripture and tradition separate them in a way that moves counter to the recent work of the World Council of Churches of Christ in affirming the unity of Scripture and tradition; it also runs counter to much recent biblical criticism, which recognizes the ignorance and misguided zeal that often helped to shape the biblical witness as well.

Furthermore, the 1988 theological statement clearly describes tradition, experience, and reason as being subservient to Scripture, in that each is described largely in relation to Scripture, with frequent reference to scriptural truth and norms.[27] Despite the examples given here, the picture is somewhat ambiguous because some credence is given in the 1988 statement to the mediation of God's grace that is possible through all four elements of the quadrilateral. Perhaps the best summary of the position of the document is found in the conclusion of the section on doctrinal guidelines:

> In theological reflection, the resources of tradition, experience, and reason are integral to our study of scripture without displacing its primacy for faith and practice. These four sources—making distinctive contributions, yet all finally working together—guide our quest as United Methodists for a vital and appropriate Christian witness.[28]

A fifth shift between the 1972 and 1988 theological statements is that toward Christocentricism. Less attention is given to the triune God, and more to God revealed in Christ. The frequent references to Jesus Christ are evidence of this shift, plus some subtle change of wording at points. One example is that the complex texture of the biblical witness as "memories, images, and hopes" is removed from the 1972 statement, and the biblical witness is spoken of primarily as revealing Jesus Christ, or the way by which "the living Christ meets us" and we "are convinced that Jesus Christ is the living Word of God."[29] Another subtle change is in the concluding words of both documents where they speak of the purpose of the theological task. The 1972 statement spoke of the task "to understand our faith in God's love, known in Jesus Christ," whereas the 1988 statement speaks of the task "to understand the love of God given in Jesus Christ."[30] The subtle difference between the words *known* and *given* suggests a shift to the idea that God is revealed only in Jesus Christ. Though the new statement does not deny other forms of revelation, it deemphasizes these considerably. Such a shift has considerable implications for the Christian relationships with other religious traditions, particularly Judaism.

A sixth shift with the 1988 theological statement is a self-conscious attempt to be more holistic in the approach to theology. Examples abound. The document speaks of both personal and corporate experience, love of God and neighbor, the critical and constructive roles of theology, the individual and communal dimensions of the task, the multiplicity of traditions, and the concern of theology with the poor and oppressed and with justice and peace.[31] These accents are not missing from the 1972 statement, but they are not featured so vividly. This is a movement in the direction of more holistic thinking, although the 1988 document does sometimes contradict such holistic thinking. The most obvious example of the contradiction might be the tendency to affirm the insights from the multiplicity of traditions, on the one hand, but to relativize them greatly in relation to scriptural norms on the other. In fact, some of the critical insights that have emerged from this multiplicity of traditions have been ignored in the formulation of the document, particularly in relation to scriptural interpretation and criticism. The contradictions, however, do not take away the power of the holistic thinking in the new document; it accentuates the breadth dimension of United Methodist theology.

Another shift represents somewhat less emphasis on ecumenical and interfaith commitments. More attention is given to John Wesley and other pioneers of the United Methodist movement, and a particular accent is placed on sharing our heritage in the ecumenical arena. Less emphasis is given to the ferment that comes from the ecumenical arena into United Methodism, or to the criticisms and challenges that come from the search for unity. The 1972 statement spoke of tough decisions required in the quest for agreement over whether "something truly essential is in jeopardy, something belonging not only to our own heritage but to the Christian tradition at large."[32]

Even more evident is a change in the understanding of interfaith commitments. The 1988 statement declares that God is "the Creator of all humankind," but no longer asserts that "God has been and is now working among all people."[33] The idea that God is actually working within non-Christian people has been eliminated. Likewise, the idea has been removed that people of different traditions need to work with God and one another for the "salvation, health, healing, and peace" of the planet.[34] The interfaith work described, instead, is "to be both neighbors and witnesses to all peoples."[35] Despite the strong overall similarities in the documents regarding ecumenical and interfaith attitudes, these changes point to a subtle shift in perspective.

The last shift relates to some of the others already discussed—namely, the move away from acknowledging problems and critiques that emerge in theological dialogue. The impetus to reflect critically on the faith tradition and to respond to contradictions is not featured. But problems often do emerge in interpreting Scripture, in adjudicating contradictions among the four sources of the quadrilateral, in responding to critiques that come from the multiplicity of traditions, in responding to the challenges of persons from different cultural and gender communities, and in dealing with issues that surface in ecumenical and interfaith dialogue. One example of the deemphasis of such problems is found in the description of the Bible in the 1988 theological statement. The Bible is said to express "the fundamental unity of God's revelation as received and experienced by people in the diversity of their own lives."[36] This statement of unity is made without acknowledging the major tensions and debates within the canon itself, as well as in the interpretations of the canon. The 1988 statement seems to present a simpler picture of our theological task than is possible if we are to take seriously the challenges that are before us.

Primary attention has been given in this analysis to the shifting emphases in the two theological statements drafted in 1972 and 1988. In these two statements, we can easily witness the dynamic of theological constancy and fluidity. The mission statement is a new addition to the denomination's study documents, but it represents some of the same patterns as the new theological statement. It tends, for example, to follow a normative approach to theology by articulating basic beliefs from which decisions about the mission of the church flow. The purpose of the statement is described as: "Not to offer a specific program but to set forth as clearly as possible the gospel of grace as it impels us to evangelize and serve the world which God in Christ 'so loved.' "[37] Like the theological statement, the mission statement appeals to history for a definition of the theological agenda, and the theological method is largely an applied approach. The document itself is not strictly an applied approach to theology, because both the beliefs and practices of the historical and contemporary churches are presented, and both give rise to theological and missional insight. The missional agenda of the past, however, is put forth much more fully than the missional agenda for today. More important, the existence of separate theological and missional statements, produced by two different commissions, is revealing. The message is that doctrine and mission are separable, more separable than one would expect from a church in which "practical divinity" has been a watchword. The two commissions did consult, but the positioning of the mission statement outside *The Book of Discipline* may suggest a derivative relationship, as does the organization of the mission statement itself.

Some other commonalities between the theological and

mission documents should be noted. Certainly, the mission statement is also holistic in its approach to theology. It draws from many sources in the Christian tradition and from both theory and practice; it argues for both individual and corporate transformation, and it speaks of various means of grace.

Like the theological statement, the mission statement makes fairly general statements regarding ecumenism, speaking of "cooperation and communion with the many authentic Christian communities."[38] Surprisingly, the statement gives even less attention to interfaith relations. The theme is that we "witness to all persons about the Lordship of Jesus Christ," but to this is added the idea that "we respect the integrity of others." The idea is summarized with these words: "As religious traditions interact, we are called to listen with sensitivity to those of differing faith while presenting Christ in the spirit of Christ."[39]

Again, as in the theological statement, the document is more clear about the importance of listening, caring for, and respecting people of different traditions than it is about responding to the problems and challenges raised by the differences. Similarly, the affirmations of inclusiveness and diversity deal more forthrightly with the variety of needs, responsibilities, and expressions of faith than with the fundamental challenges to faith that are inevitably raised by diverse peoples' taking one another seriously.[40] This is not to say that the mission statement is purely naive; it does articulate clearly many of the problems in today's world and the challenges and difficulties that lie ahead. It also articulates the double need for the formation and transformation of the church and for the church's going into the world.[41]

And so, The United Methodist Church has two new statements for theological reflection, continuing the tradition that United Methodist people are continually doing theology. One can even argue that the documents are practical and speculate about some of the practical problems that gave rise to the commissioning of the statements and to their particular shapes. Certainly, two influences on the statements were the conflicts that had emerged from the differences in the church itself and the Christian struggle for identity in a rapidly changing and pluralistic world. These two statements did, indeed, arise from practical needs, and their value is being measured by the potential practical effects. The statements also continue the United Methodist tradition of discipline, rising out of the organizational structures of the church and offering two disciplined statements, one of which will be included in *The Book of Discipline*. They represent both the fluidity and constancy of the United Methodist theological tradition, but I have argued here that both appeal more to constancy than to fluidity. Also, the two statements represent the connection. They were commissioned by the General Conference, appointed by the Council of Bishops, written by committees, responded to by numerous groups within the church, reformed by a legislative committee, and adopted by the General Conference. The process of communal theologizing seems to be alive and well. And finally, the move toward holism reinforces the breadth and universal-mindedness of the denomination's theology. The question now is where do the United Methodist traditions of theological reflection, and some of the recent developments in those traditions, lead the church in regard to the teaching office.

The Future of the Teaching Office in United Methodist Tradition

The church has not put forth a clear mandate for the teaching office in its theological and missional documents. In fact, the missional statement defines the mission of the church in terms of proclamation, evangelism, incorporation, and servanthood.[42] Certainly, all of these can be related to teaching, but none is explicitly teaching. If one adds to this observation the insight of Thomas Langford that neither bishops nor pastors are given clear authority by *The Book of Discipline* to teach, then the teaching office seems shaky. Langford argues that the teaching role of the bishops is ambiguous, with little explicit teaching delegated. And the teaching role of ordained ministers is communicated only indirectly. (See chap. 3 of this book.) Furthermore, neither the annual conferences nor the General Conference have a clear understanding and will to perform the teaching functions delegated to them. This does leave a mess. We have no specific individuals delegated, and the corporate bodies do not generally take up their delegated responsibilities to teach and to do theology. So what challenge may be identified for the future of the church's teaching?

One set of challenges comes from the practices of theological reflection within the United Methodist tradition. Since theological reflection is a central part of teaching, these practices have much to say about the role of the teaching office in The United Methodist Church. The first challenge named above is to do theology continually, even while the church is moving. This is the challenge to continue to reflect theologically on issues even after decisions are made; it is the challenge to see theology as a dynamic unfinished movement belonging to all times and places of the church. The second challenge is to welcome various motivations for doing theology and for teaching. Whether motivated by wonder, fear, or frustration with the current situation, all provide the occasion for thinking seriously about our faith. The third challenge to teaching and theologizing is to recognize that celebration is part of the process. Creating reasons and opportunities for genuine celebration contributes significantly to the teaching act.

Another set of challenges for teaching comes from the marks of United Methodist theology. Teaching needs to be practical because theology is practical. The theological content of teaching needs to be shaped not only by doctrinal traditions or by Scripture and other texts, but also by a concern for practical divinity, what we described earlier as a concern for genuine Christianity in the lives of believers. Both the methods and the content of teaching need to be shaped by questions such as: What kind of teaching would contribute to the growth of discipleship in this group of people? What are the critical issues in the church and world, and how do they shape the selection of theological content?

If the second mark of United Methodist theology is discipline, then teaching needs to be done in a disciplined manner and for the sake of discipline. The word *discipline* in United Methodist traditions rarely has referred to "good behavior"; it has referred, instead, to the organization and guidance of beliefs and actions. What does this mean for teaching? Certainly, the life of the church should be organized in order to maximize the possibilities for teaching. Both church structures and church programs need to contribute opportunities for carrying on the theological tasks. Also, opportunities for teaching need to be sought within all of the structures of the church, including governing bodies, evangelism work areas, church choirs, and the like. This would include ongoing, disciplined theological work, such as that done by the theological and mission commissions appointed by the Council of Bishops, but it would also include ongoing, disciplined theological work done in local churches as they reflect on the official documents in *The Book of Discipline* and on Scripture, tradition, experience, and reason. Certainly, too, annual conferences and the General Conference are challenged to seek ways to engage in disciplined theological reflection alongside their decision-making, and as part of their decision-making. Finally, and most important, respect for the discipline of the Holy Spirit would suggest that all teaching takes place in the context of a prayerful sense of God's presence.

The United Methodist tradition of fluidity and constancy further challenges the church to take seriously the historical traditions that have brought us to this point without literalizing them or making them the absolute test of faith. Those graced with the responsibilities of the teaching office have a responsibility to transmit the traditions, but to do so in a way that is open to new interpretations and applications of the traditions as well as to new revelations from God and the formation of new traditions.

On the importance of continuity with the Scripture and historical tradition, the 1988 theological statement is very explicit. Both the theological and mission statements demonstrate how this continuity can be achieved, and they serve as excellent source documents for studying the historical and biblical traditions. On the importance of fluidity in the theological task, the new documents offer less guidance. The very existence of those two theological commissions, however, and the creation of the two reports in the midst of considerable informal dialogue and revision would suggest a model of how the fluidity can be encouraged. In fact, the formation of the standing legislative committee on Faith and Mission for General Conference will ensure a continuation of active reflection on the documents themselves and on the issues related to our theological task as Christians.

Implications for the curriculum resources of the church include the need to offer access to the historical and biblical traditions as well as to experience and reason. They need to offer processes for dynamic theological reflection that encourage persons to take the historical traditions seriously as well as to wrestle with the new insights and critiques that emerge. They need to support people in forming and reforming their faith, and to offer guidance to teachers whose role is to sponsor persons and communities as they journey in the fluid and constant Christian tradition.

The fourth mark that we named in United Methodist theology is connection. Since this challenge is similar to some of those already named, I will intensify earlier suggestions. The challenge involves more than gathering people into groups, committees, and governing bodies to talk about theology. It entails creating a connectional system for teaching that (1) clearly designates teaching responsibility to particular leaders and specific bodies of the church; (2) continues to designate theological and missional study commissions with the expectation that they will create opportunities to broaden their dialogue through the whole church; and (3) holds bishops and all representative ordained ministers accountable to teach in their respective contexts and to guide and support the teaching connections of the church. Besides a structure to support the connections of teaching, we also need an attitude as a denomination to support a conciliar process in which "the collective wisdom of living Christian pastors, teachers, and people" is the means by which we guard and guide our ongoing communal life.[43] If we develop such a conciliar attitude, we will shy away from any tendency to expect bishops, theological professors, representative ministers, or theological commissions to be the guards and guides of the denomination. Instead, these people will be expected to offer their unique contributions to the communal process of teaching and doing theology.

Another mark in United Methodist theology challenges us to keep our sights broad when we consider what kind of action and reflection to include in teaching. Every dimension of our lives is within the purview of theology. Every action and belief is subject to theological reflection. To separate theology from historical witness and doctrine, from the life of the individual Christian, or from the social structures and interactions in the world deadens the life of theology and limits its influence. Every church body has responsibility for doing theology and engaging teaching. Teaching in any context needs to be holistic.

It should be concerned with the perspectives, gifts, and urgent needs that emerge from the multiplicity of communities in the church and world. Teaching should take seriously the idea that God is revealed in all times and places, and it should draw upon the sources of Scripture, tradition, experience, and reason to ensure breadth and depth in our efforts.

If we take this breadth factor seriously, we will look not just to bishops and professors of Bible and theology for consultation, but to persons engaged in various forms of social mission and ministerial practice as well. If we take the breadth factor seriously, we will seek broad representation in all local and general church bodies, and we will ensure leadership rotation so that fresh perspectives and new questions continue to enliven the church's theology.

The mark of universal-mindedness reminds us that even our United Methodist pastors, teachers, and people are not sufficient for theological dialogue and action. The theological task needs to take place in the midst of ecumenical dialogue and action and the search for Christian unity. The theological task needs to take place in the midst of interfaith relationships for mutual sharing and learning and for common work on global issues. And the theological task needs full participation from all ethnic, cultural, and national communities of the globe. At all levels of church life and in any part of the world, United Methodists can seek ways to join with other peoples in theological action and reflection. Christian mission with other Christians and global mission with people of other religious traditions can signal our desire to work with God and other people for the sake of the planet. Curriculum resources can provide the stories and art of other traditions and communities to expand our awareness. Local churches can reach out to people of other traditions in their communities.

Such are the challenges that lie before The United Methodist Church in reforming the teaching office and in giving new life to the ministry of teaching. If we look only to the new theological and missional documents as blueprints for teaching, we have limited guidance, but if we look to these documents within the historical traditions, contemporary issues, and lively communities of discourse that produced them, we will find much to guide us.

The documents taken alone support a socialization approach to teaching that has evangelism and incorporation as its primary goals (understood as inviting people to Christian commitment and incorporating them into the Body of Christ). Teaching would focus on the historical texts and practices of the church and encourage persons to interpret and act on these in relation to their situations in the contemporary world. Critical reflection and reformation of the tradition would be limited. So would theological reflection on the contemporary world. Less attention would be given to the pilgrimage quality of Christian life, and more to the quest for truth and its application. Less passion would be invested in ecumenical and interfaith relationships, and more would be invested in United Methodist Christian identity. A strong Christian identity would be passed on, in fact, and this would be done through the whole life of the church. It would be done with respect and awareness of differences, but with an effort to avoid the possibility that these differences might lead to radical transformation of the identity itself.

The same documents, when seen within the communal and dynamic contexts in which they were formed, reinforce and enlarge the significance of the marks of United Methodist theology for our teaching. In this larger framework they may help United Methodists understand and proclaim their faith and find their identity in the midst of a rapidly changing and pluralistic world. They may help us discover many resources in our historical tradition to guide our own faith journeys and to offer to the larger church and to the world. They may serve as our contribution to the church's persistent quest for unity in the midst of its diversity. They can remind us of the multiplicity of traditions that may contribute to our fullness and enrich our unity. If we take the marks of the United Methodist theological enterprise seriously through our teaching, we as a people may become more self-conscious of who we are, more aware of the dynamic quality of any theological statement we or others make, more humble in relation to our own theological affirmations, and more eager to participate in the ongoing formulation and reformulation of our theological task.

NOTES

1. "Our Doctrinal Heritage," *Daily Christian Advocate* VII (May 2, 1988) 6:248.

2. Ibid.

3. *The Book of Discipline of The United Methodist Church 1984* (Nashville: The United Methodist Publishing House, 1984), p. 19. Hereafter referred to as *Discipline*.

4. Ibid., p. 25.

5. Ibid. p. 78.

6. Ibid., p. 41.

7. Ibid.

8. *Daily Christian Advocate*, p. 254.

9. *Discipline*, p. 49.

10. See *Discipline*, pp. 78-81, and *Daily Christian Advocate*, pp. 254-56.

11. *Discipline*, p. 19. The theme of organic union appears on this same page, where the union of The Methodist Church and The

Evangelical United Brethren Church is seen as obedience to God's will that the people of God be one.

12. See *Daily Christian Advocate,* VII (May 7, 1988) 11:7, 12.

13. Ibid.

14. *Daily Christian Advocate,* May 2, 1988, p. 247.

15. *Discipline,* p. 73.

16. See ibid., pp. 71-72.

17. See ibid., p. 78; and *Daily Christian Advocate,* May 2, 1988, p. 254.

18. See *Daily Christian Advocate,* May 2, 1988, pp. 247-53, and *Discipline,* p. 41.

19. *Daily Christian Advocate,* May 2, 1988, p. 255.

20. These references in the 1972 theological statement can be found respectively on the following pages of *Discipline*: 41, 42, 50, 54, 71, and 78.

21. Ibid., p. 252.

22. Ibid., p. 253.

23. Ibid., p. 50.

24. References in the two documents can be found in "Historical Background," *Discipline,* pp. 50-53, and *Daily Christian Advocate,* May 2, 1988, p. 254.

25. *Daily Christian Advocate,* May 2, 1988, p. 255.

26. Ibid.

27. See ibid., pp. 255-56.

28. Ibid., p. 256.

29. Compare the two statements on Scripture for subtle changes of emphasis in regard to God's self-disclosures and in regard to the nature and function of the Bible itself. The particular phrases cited here are found in *Discipline,* p. 78, and *Daily Christian Advocate,* May 2, 1988, p. 254.

30. *Discipline,* p. 85; *Daily Christian Advocate,* May 2, 1988, p. 257.

31. The particular references to the phrases listed are found respectively in the following passages: *Daily Christian Advocate,* May 2, 1988, pp. 250, 253, 255; 250; 253; 253-54; and 255.

32. *Discipline,* p. 84.

33. *Daily Christian Advocate,* May 2, 1988, p. 256; and *Discipline,* p. 84.

34. *Discipline,* p. 84.

35. *Daily Christian Advocate,* May 2, 1988, p. 256.

36. Ibid., p. 255.

37. "The Mission of The United Methodist Church," *Daily Christian Advocate,* Advance Edition C, VII (February 25, 1988): C-15 and C-16.

38. Ibid., p. C-21.

39. Ibid., p. C-22.

40. See ibid., p. C-21.

41. See ibid., pp. C-19 and C-20.

42. See ibid., p. C-22.

43. *Discipline,* p. 41.

IV.
VOICES THAT NEED TO
BE HEARD

The discussion on teaching authority through the centuries has always been influenced by voices, issues, and ideas that were not central to the way the church currently understood its ministry and mission. In some instances these voices had been oppressed; the contribution of laity is one example. In other instances they existed at the margins of church life. The contributions of mission churches may be illustrative. In still other situations they reflected new bodies of knowledge that affected both the content and the method of teaching. The insights of psychology during the past one hundred years, for example, have significantly influenced the way we teach.

The three chapters that follow reveal limits and problems in older views on the authority of teaching in the church. They confront us with the necessity to rethink what does function authoritatively for a church that seeks to engage in teaching ministries with understandings that speak to the experience of all people today. Two of the chapters that follow identify disparities in the efforts of the church to communicate the gospel to women and to people who did not share the church's dominant cultural experience. Another chapter explores insights from contemporary research and writing about ways people teach and learn. The following questions may help focus your own thoughts about the issues these writers raise:

1. In what ways does each chapter challenge your assumptions about the way teaching occurs in The United Methodist Church, in the congregation, and beyond the local church?

2. In what ways could these voices strengthen the church's teaching?

Chapter 6

The Authority to Teach in Cross-Cultural Contexts

Joseph V. Crockett

The experience of racial/ethnic cultures with the institutions and policies of the dominant culture in the United States (including those of the church) leads their members to approach any discussion of authority with caution. They recognize that the authority as practiced by dominant cultural institutions has sanctioned both revolutionary actions of liberation and oppressive actions of injustice. Part of their caution arises from the variety of ways in which the concept of authority may be understood.

Authority involves the capacity to exercise dominance through the rights and responsibilities of an office or position. The authority of bishops, for example, is sanctioned by the political processes of an election and the liturgical activity of consecration. The "authority" of office or position is limited structurally to specific times and places. If a person chooses to leave an acquired position, the authority he or she possesses would cease to exist. The "authority" of an office or position may be used coercively or persuasively, autocratically or beneficially. Whatever approach a person might take to the authority received by virtue of an office or position, however,

129

much of his or her attention is directed to the exercise of power and control.

In contrast, authority may also be viewed in terms of relationships. Relational authority is often evident in the interactions of a parent and a child, a principal and a teacher, or an employer and an employee. Relational forms of authority involve the exercise of control and power as well, but the focus is on mutuality and interdependence, growth and liberation.

The Christian community has articulated different views of authority over the centuries. These may be distinguished as hierarchical, communal, and missionary approaches to the exercise of authority. Hierarchical perspectives locate authority in persons such as a pope or a king, in precedent perspectives and actions, and in doctrines and traditions that are valued more than current experience or understandings. Communal authority is located in the collaborative processes of institutional or social life. In the church, for example, it is exercised through the decisions of believers who make judgments that guide and govern the common life of the community.

A third view of authority—also derived from the scriptures—is related to the church's mission. In the Gospel of Mark 6:7-13 (see also Matt. 28:16-20; Luke 24:27) direct authorization and empowerment of the church is given by Jesus to the apostles. Jesus connects the giving of authority with the apostle's responsibility to heal, teach, and cast out demons in his name. Authority is given for the purpose of inviting people to deepen their relationship with God. It sanctions and mobilizes the invitation to all peoples to believe with their minds, trust with their hearts, and obey with their lives the will of God. Missionary authority is located in the leadership of Jesus the Christ of God. It is exercised in love for the service of reconciling humanity with the creator God.

The transformative nature of missionary authority may be seen in the actions of the late Reverend Doctor Martin Luther

King, Jr. When King rejected the unjust laws of discrimination through acts of civil disobedience, the laws failed to have authority for or over him. However, inasmuch as King accepted the authority of Jesus Christ, he found himself empowered to transcend the inconsistencies, contradictions, and injustices of the European-American community and love its members despite their involvement in prejudicial and oppressive activity.

Although authority is expressed in a variety of human interactions, the ethical exercise of authority is most evident in the missionary character of the church's ministry. The missionary understanding of authority asserts the participation of racial/ethnic cultures in the exploration of the function of authority in relation to the rules and regulations, traditions, and personalities to be found in any community. However, it is the personality of Jesus the Christ of God that gives the church its clues for what its mission is. From this perspective, *authority may be defined as the legitimate influence of the church exercised in efforts of service for the work of humanity's reconciliation with God*. The source of authority is Jesus the Christ of God, whose ministry marks the rules, traditions, beliefs, and leadership of the church that seek to proclaim his mind and mission to all peoples.

Even this definition of authority has limits. No discussion of authority can be engaged without recognizing that it occurs in the context of historical and cultural relativity. An understanding of authority must be viewed through the lens of particular world views. Subsequently, conversations about authority and the teaching office of the church must include a critical analysis of its historical and cultural context.

Edward B. Tylor's omnibus definition of culture has shaped and continues to chart the course for the critical analyses of the term. Tylor wrote in *Primitive Culture* that "culture or Civilization, taken in its wide ethnographic sense, is that complex whole which includes knowledge, belief, art, morals, law, custom, and any other capabilities and habits acquired by man as a member of society.''[1]

According to Tylor, there are four primary characteristics of culture. It consists, first of all, of patterns of configuration, which may include the structure of language or the forms of dance. Second, culture involves the regularities of human behavior; for example, culture includes the customs, rituals, habits, and laws of social groupings. Third, culture is relational, not individual. And fourth, culture is acquired, not inherited. In addition to these four characteristics, Tylor's definition also implies that culture is created by human collectives or social groups, has a repetitious nature, and continues in time through the customs, rituals, and practices of groups and institutions.

Cultural characteristics, patterns, and forms can be observed in the church's teaching. Teaching is always couched in cultural categories and forms, and the authority for teaching is always derived from and expressed through cultural configurations and patterns. A common metaphor of teaching, for example, compares the learner to a receptacle and the teacher to a fountain of knowledge and truth. The message in this metaphor emphasizes the role and responsibility of teachers to transmit their knowledge into the "container mind" of learners. This metaphor both gives rise to and extends the views of teaching and learning that are deeply rooted in Western cultural traditions. It gathers support from and gives credence to the hierarchical structures and relationships to be found in much of the Christian education in the society of the United States. It is not a relevant metaphor, however, for teaching in African-American or Native American cultures.

In a pluralistic church and society, diverse cultural forms and patterns often lead to tension or conflict. Thomas Kochman, in *Black and White Styles in Conflict,* explores, for example, differences in the ways European-Americans and African-Americans express anger.

> When opponents become angry and engage in verbal dispute, whites feel that they are reducing the danger of violence by keeping the antagonists apart. This is based on their view that struggle is basically divisive and that public arguments, if not stopped, will inevitably escalate into violence.[2]

In contrast, a common African-American perspective affirms the anger that underlies conflict as healthy and a necessary part of human interaction. Conflict here is understood as struggle. Life is a struggle. This affirmative view of the anger in conflict illuminates why many African-Americans refer to the civil rights movement of the mid 1950s and 1960s as "The Struggle."

Tylor's definition of culture has contributed to the development of two distinct, yet interrelated, strands of thought. The first concerns cultural patterns. In describing culture as patterns, Kroeber and Kluckholn wrote:

> Culture is not behavior nor the investigation of behavior in all its concrete completeness. Part of culture consists in norms or standards of behavior. Still another part consists in ideologies justifying or rationalizing certain selected ways of behavior. . . . Every culture includes broad general principles of selectivity and ordering . . . in terms of which patterns of and for and about behavior in very varied areas of culture content are reducible to parsimonious generalizations.[3]

Irving Hallowell, in expanding the work of Kroeber and Kluckholn, has insisted that culture ought not to be equated with learning or the intentional transmission of behavior.[4] Yet, all three scholars recognize the fact that culture is one of the necessary conditions underlying any and all forms of communication and social transmission. Cultural patterns may

133

be described further in terms of simple or complex levels of operation. Examples of simple levels of cultural patterning include dress, dance, and folklore. Complex levels of cultural patterning would include assumptions underlying social, political, educational, economic, religious, language, and legal structures and systems.

A review of attitudes and policies of educational agencies in the United States clearly demonstrates that the exercise of authority has centered on patterns of dominance and control. The experience of these patterns lies behind the cautiousness among people in the racial/ethnic cultures in the United States when the church begins to talk of teaching authority. A glimpse of their experience with the history of the dominant culture's view of authority is presented below because the attitudes and practices of churches in their education paralleled the attitudes and practices of the larger European-American society.

For racial/ethnic cultures in the United States, educational choices and opportunities have been more limited than for European-Americans. Let us consider the experience of the Native American. Under the guise of religious uplift and social reform, the United States Congress in 1819 enacted legislation to introduce Native Americans to "the habits and arts of civilization."[5] Educational policies were later enacted to separate Native Americans from their homeland and their tribes. The aim of European-Americans in educating the Native Americans was clearly for them to "walk the white man's road."

Or let us take a look at the participation of Asian-Americans in the educational enterprise of the United States. In San Francisco in the 1870s, sentiments were high enough to keep Chinese students from attending public schools. The San Francisco school board ruled "that our children should not be placed in any position where their youthful impression may be affected by associations with pupils of the Mongolian race."[6]

Several denominations held special classes for Asians in the late 1890s and early 1900s to teach the Chinese and Japanese immigrants the English language. In return, the Asians were invited to become Christians.

Spanish-speaking cultures—including Mexicans, Cubans, Puerto Ricans, Central and South Americans, and others—were not generally classified as non-white by the United States government. Consequently, national educational policies and strategies for the separation of the Spanish-speaking cultures from other European-Americans had to be rationalized on different terms. Thus the dominant culture justified their separation on the basis of instructional needs. One example occurred after the 1954 Supreme Court ruling concerning the desegregation of schools when educational districts in the Southwest integrated their schools by mixing Spanish-speaking groups with African-Americans. These school districts thereby avoided integrating blacks and whites as well as further mixing whites with Hispanics.

Despite the explicit and exaggerated forms of cross-cultural oppression, African-Americans transmitted and renewed specific cultural patterns across the generations even when their social structures inhibited them from fully functioning. A typical example may be seen in the "strings attached" to white gifts to black colleges, effectively prohibiting the schools from engaging in politics and policies opposed to dominant cultural positions. Two institutions that experienced this reality were Hampton Institute and Tuskegee Institute.

A second implication from Tylor's definition of culture has to do with the meaning and significance of social structures. A. R. Radcliffe-Brown has made the point that if culture is "a network or system of social relations including persistent social groups and differentiated social classes and social roles," then "each structural system is a functional unity in which all the component parts contribute in a harmonious way to its existence and continuity."[7]

Raymond W. Firth pushes the consequences of this line of thinking to its logical conclusion. If the social relations of people can be described only "by reference to the reciprocal behavior" of the persons involved, then social structures can be understood only through descriptions of "the patterns of behavior to which individuals and groups conform in their dealings with one another."[8]

From this perspective, commodities and products are the direct consequences of social relations. Curriculum is a specific expression of social relations. Answers to questions such as "What should be taught?" and "Who should decide what to teach?" and "How is it to be distributed?" illustrate the social relations to which persons and groups conform. The book and educational resources chosen, as well as the processes used and the theories designated as "truth," are all consequences of social relations.

> The choice of particular content and ways of approaching it in schools is related both to existing relations of domination and to struggles to alter these relations. . . . Though the ties that link curricula to the inequalities and social struggles of our social formation are very complicated . . . nevertheless, the social relations exist.[9]

For example, in one dominant approach of Christian curriculum publishing, information is to be presented for dialogue and discussion. The approach appeals to the individual's thinking capacity almost exclusively. This strategy assumes that if a person's mind is informed with reasonable information, right actions will naturally follow. Such a strategy does not account for the diversity of approaches to learning to be found in people. It does not acknowledge the differences in cultural learning styles.

Due to these limitations, minority racial/ethnic writers and educators have attempted to alter this approach to curriculum.

136

They have struggled to unify accurate thinking with faithful action. They have sought to integrate issues of personal discipleship and psychological well-being with issues and concerns of corporate discipleship and social responsibility. The difficulties they have encountered may be traced in part to the exercise of the church's authority in and through decisions made in an ecology of social relations, emphasizing majority dominance and hierarchical decision making.

"Cross-culture" designates the interaction of two or more cultural patterns or cultural social relations with the individual or group and the environment. In the United States, the phenomenon of cross-cultural relationships is significantly related to the voluntary and involuntary immigration of diverse cultural and ethnic groups. The cross-cultural character of the nation's society means that questions regarding how cultures relate to, accommodate, assimilate, and search for other alternative social structures cannot be avoided. Questions about the exercise of authority are among the most critical in cross-cultural societies.

Authority has both constructive and destructive potential. It can both provide for continuity and the empowerment of people in a society and subordinate some cultures to others. The latter pattern has dominated the experience of the various racial/ethnic cultures in the United States and contributes to their being on guard for clues to the destructive employment of authority in the institutions and social relations in which they find themselves.

On what basis, therefore, can The United Methodist Church or any other Christian denomination claim authority to teach in cross-cultural settings? How can The United Methodist Church teach in cross-cultural settings in ways that legitimate the diversity of its cultural composition? The recommendations below grow out of the above discussion. They involve a reconstructive approach to the way Christian education authority and culture interact in the effort to achieve the church's educational aims.

1. *The United Methodist Church must realign its social relations with regard to the office of teaching.* Racial/ethnic cultures must be provided with the skills to discover, critique, and reconstruct their cultural patterns and social structures in the light of the mission and ministry of the church. It is not just or equitable for European-Americans to decide for racial/ethnic groups what content they need to learn. Neither is it ethical for European-Americans to decide for racial/ethnic groups how the gospel of Jesus Christ would critique their cultural forms and patterns. When social relations are realigned with the mission of the church, the democratic principle of one vote per person is dismissed for the sake of the gospel.

2. *Invite all cultures to share, rehearse, and exchange their folklore, art, rituals, customs, and patterns of interaction in the educational enterprise.* At present the frames of reference for the teaching office of the church are culturally biased. European-American culture is the standard of measurement against which the folklore, art, rituals, customs, and patterns of interaction occur. For example, art in curriculum today continues to depict biblical characters as European-Americans, and the mission and ministry of Christian discipleship continues to look more like a prototype of the democratic platform. The teaching office of the church, to be viable in cross-cultural situations, must expand its horizons and critique its assumptions.

3. *Empower all cultures, particularly racial/ethnic cultures, to cultivate, value, and teach their heritages to their communities.* This task involves the handing on of a heritage and the recognition that new generations are themselves the originating contexts and environments for subsequent generations. This task is central to the revisioning of the relationship of racial/ethnic cultures between their self-identity and public

policy and action. It becomes the basis for their full participation in a cross-cultural society.

4. *Educate and teach for racial/ethnic cultural cohesion, autonomy, and assertiveness.* To undertake this task would mean a reversal of most teaching philosophies and strategies in the church's education. Most education philosophies in the church and the larger society continue to use and aim for the great "melting pot" theory, which has never taken seriously the gifts of racial/ethnic cultures to the whole social fabric. The goal of this task is to help racial/ethnic communities draw upon the resources of their own heritages and experiences for the decisions they make in their interactions with the rest of the church and society.

The concern for authority, inevitably, is in part a concern for control. The strength of that concern is related to the continuity of meaning, truth, value, and experience. The danger of authority as control occurs when authority asserts the primacy of one particular cultural perspective of meaning, truth, value, or experience over another. The use of authority can become pernicious when it establishes primacy on the basis of cultural dominance. The discussion of teaching authority is relevant at this point in the church's history, because if approached with a sensitivity to the contributions of all cultures to the church's education, the ministry and mission of the church will reflect more adequately the fullness of God's creation.

NOTES

1. Edward B. Tylor, *Primitive Culture: Researches into the Development of Mythology, Philosophy, Religion, Art, and Custom,* vol. 1 (Gloucester, Mass.: Smith, 1958), p. 1.

2. Thomas Kochman, *Black and White Styles in Conflict* (Chicago: University of Chicago Press, 1981), p. 58.

3. Alfred L. Kroeber and Clyde Kluckhohn, *Culture: A Critical Review of Concepts and Definitions* (Cambridge, Mass.: Harvard University Press, 1952), p. 185.

4. See Irving Hallowell, "Personality, Culture, and Society in Behavioral Evolution," in *Psychology: A Study of a Science,* ed. Sigmund Koch (New York: McGraw-Hill, 1963), p. 492.

5. Stephan Thernstrom, ed., *Harvard Encyclopedia of American Ethnic Groups* (Cambridge, Mass.: Harvard University Press, 1980), p. 312.

6. Ibid., p. 159.

7. A. R. Radcliffe-Brown, *Structure and Function in Primitive Society* (London: Cohen and West, 1952), p. 195.

8. Raymond W. Firth, *Elements of Social Organization* (London: Watts, 1951), p. 198.

9. Michael W. Apple, *Teachers and Texts* (New York: Routledge and Kegan Paul, 1986), pp. 84ff.

Chapter 7

The Heart's Warmth Is Not So Strange:
A Feminist Paradigm

The feminist critique of culture is shared by brothers and
sisters who perceive that our patriarchal cultural heritage and its
institutions serve androcentric ends. They find this male
centeredness detrimental to women and the exercise of human
community. They believe a new paradigm of human interaction
is required. This feminist challenge calls for conversion and
"conscientization" to social perspectives that are inclusive and
holistic. It affirms a transformation of culture that asserts the
fullness of womanhood and moves toward the free participation
of every human being. It seeks a social-symbolic order that
overcomes oppositional consciousness. It values multiple
perspectives among people who discern together what is caring,
right, and/or just.

Persons familiar with feminist scholarship know that there is
debate over the visions and strategies that make up this
paradigm shift. Protracted idealogues characterize the efforts of
feminist scholars in religion and theology. Some voices are
more strident than others, and these voices reflect different
backgrounds, personalities, and political contexts. Their ideas
mix with androcentric language, symbol systems, and religious
structures in many ways. Some are called revisionists. Others

are called reconstructionists, reformers, radicals, or revolutionaries. All participate, however, in the feminist spoken/written/ created interrelations of a newly forming paradigm. Their work is not independent of the knower, the language, or the interpretive community.

When United Methodist feminists hear leaders in the church calling for the establishment of a teaching office that would regularly and thoroughly assess what the church teaches, the contours of patriarchal images and language loom large. They know that much of our social interaction consists of constructing "right thinking." They recognize that institutions shape our perceptions with forms compatible to those who authorize "responsible" behavior. They realize that policy makers for institutions are held accountable by and for the dominant tradition. They also know that when members raise voices that expose and make an impact on the identity and order of the dominant reign, issues regarding the legitimacy of their ideas and views are raised. Historical perspective can help us to see that in times of cultural crisis questions of interpretation become central. What shall be the interpretation of and about the future of the institution? The interest in the legitimacy of those interpretations reveals a concern for the control of new thinking at work in the process of change. "Teachings" move to center stage when the interpretation of institutional values and beliefs matter. Since new inquiry in changing circumstances raises new sets of meaning in institutional and social transformation, feminists know they are challenging a dominant Eurocentric patriarchal-hierarchical paradigm. For feminists committed to Christian faith, the new interest in reclaiming a teaching office raises questions about the motivation behind it. Is it an attempt to turn back the clock to try to recover the stability of a faith time now passed? Or could it be an invitation to give thoughtfulness to the importance of teaching how to think and act in love and freedom in new ways?

Feminists care about being a communicative community engaged in the task of discerning the structures of domination and oppression threatening needed transformations.

Since the ever-present male power has been experienced as a voice of domination, the feminist instinctively is moved to question what in the wider social context prompts this need for authoritative teaching. Possible answers are easy to find.

1. The power and prestige of mainstream Protestant churches, which were part of the establishment's influence (WASP male) in the social and economic life of many North American communities, have waned. As educators, we know a Protestant hegemony once influenced all levels of instruction. Agencies such as the YWCA, the YMCA, Sunday school, vacation Bible school, summer camps, and youth fellowships spread an ethos of knowledge rooted in biblical meanings. Changing cultural patterns have left little authority to religious groups. It is little wonder, then, that the "disestablished" must reflect on the establishment of teaching authority.

2. "Back to basics" is a part of the current cultural crisis rhetoric, directed at educational institutions in our society. It is a plea that also emerges in the churches. It is based on the hope that we may return to the time when we all thought we knew what teaching the faith authoritatively was. It is evident in the recent General Conference decision to reduce the function of tradition, experience, and reason and to make the teaching of Scripture primary—a move supporting a biblical hermeneutic of male salvation history. A feminist cannot support such an effort to return to a past magisterium era.

Some Reflections on the Quadrilateral

The contemporary situation requires United Methodist feminists to ask themselves whether they engage in conversations regarding how The United Methodist Church can and should teach authoritatively today. Some sisters would claim

143

that the game is the master's and accept Audre Lord's counsel that "the master's tools will never dismantle the master's house."[1] Others, however, would engage in dialogue on The United Methodist Church's guidelines for theological reflection—Scripture, tradition, experience, and reason—as sources and criteria for reflection upon the teaching office. We would approach that conversation clear about the patriarchal patterns of "saving authority," to which we will not return, and the necessity of retrieving many of the voices in our Jewish and Christian heritage who have not been heard.

Scripture. Feminists will not give up their right to read texts as women. Feminist hermeneutics have explored the inferiority, subordination, and abuse of women in the land of the patriarchs. We have discovered a counterculture within the canon and have been recovering neglected texts and reinterpreting familiar ones. Reclaiming woman from the male imagery and language has uncovered female imagery for God and released woman from the tradition of subordination. With sympathy, the tales of terror are reread and the memory of the unnamed is given care. From the texts that have shaped gender roles for generations, a new text is emerging. Authorship of textuality is a creative process through which we create structures and styles to serve. The women with new eyes do learn by studying a new complexity from the words of Scripture. And, behold, a new creation!

Tradition. Feminists will not give up the right to tell the stories women tell. Sexism has a long history as the oldest form of oppression in the world. We are looking into the past to stress an underside of tradition. Our "view from below" is uncovering autonomous women placed by ecclesiastical historians in patterns of punishment and exile. We, who are still marginal as outsiders to the mainstream, ask different questions as we relate to "the endless line of splendor." Our Christian foresisters hold potential to reveal to us what perpetuates alienation in the context of keeping and transmitting knowledge. To risk speaking both of the past and of the visions of the future as we recover tradition helps us to overcome the notion of tradition as a fixed body of knowledge to be covered. Institutions create, name, and write their traditions. Women, whom women choose, are not to be silent in our stories. They will relate us to wider contexts and communities of our lives.

Experience. Feminists will not give up their connectional conversations. Patriarchal discourse represents woman as one without authority to act unless authorized by a "father" whose permission allows disclosure. We conceive of ourselves as actually experiencing without subordination and repression. We do not deny differences or insist on unity.

Feminist consciousness requires the recognition of one's social location and how it affects one's view of reality. In coming to this consciousness, we come to challenge the two natures of interpreting human existence. We claim for women power for full engagement in being actors in our finite creation. Interaction between persons includes their gendered embodiment in time and space. Experience is not disembodied action. The witness of women's action has value. The places of women's activity are not to be valued through the eyes of others. We need not be "other" to ourselves. Male culture has required an unspoken denial of gendered difference. The female is denied the difference of her personal experience. When women differ, feminists allow them to inhabit other spaces. We do not need to deny our bodies and their locations. We are creators of a climate that may explore alternatives to assumptions, goals, and methods that serve to preserve male authority. No communicative actions should hold special privilege.

Reason. Feminists will not accept being evaluated by males in positions of isolated power. A popular conception about feminist religious thought assumes that it begins with criticism of patriarchal theology. This is not so. Feminist theology is rooted in concrete, personal, communal experience. Feminists who engage within the sexist frameworks of the ongoing life of the church struggle with their confessional commitment. We are convinced that God's way of being in the world is communal. We take seriously participation in ritual and ethics that engage the contexts of our living.

Feminists regard as highly suspicious reliance on any presuppositions that must go unchallenged. Critical scrutiny of reason needs to be brought to the "knowledge" we are to "know." Examination of this consensus and neutrality uncovers the realities of power. It is reasonable for women to ask who is the "we" who made the decision that such and such knowledge is appropriate. What are the social and ideological assumptions that make this text legitimate, while the gender, class, or race dynamics of other communities with Christian memory and experience are not transmitted? Whose reason is used to probe text and tradition? Feminists experience Eurocentric, objective logic as disenfranchising concerns for connectedness and care. Bureaucratic centralization around a center that holds at bay the articulation of different participants is not to be reasonable about the meaning of relational dialogue. Mutual concern calls for multiple voices arising from reflection and praxis.

There are Christian feminists who believe that the teaching office of the church manifests itself whenever the Holy Spirit enlivens Christians to new life and leads the church into greater wholeness of response to God's creative and redemptive activity in the world. From this perspective, reason takes place in the assembly of the people. All the voices of those who seek to be faithful to Christ through the Holy Spirit seek to speak truth to power. Inclusive participation in the global village church may not return to the alleged finality of Reformation theologies we have assumed for Protestantism. The Holy Spirit

146

of justice and love is at work outside the church as well. Feminist sisters beyond our community affect our spirituality and social witness with their testimony. All four facets of the quadrilateral interact toward our coherent faithfulness to Christ through the Holy Spirit.

Feminists are more focused on process than on product. Reciprocal recognition in who we are and where we are is our gift to the ministry of the church. This roots us in the primacy of practice. We would approach the establishment of teaching office from this stance.

Some Reflections on Authority

Feminists have a complicated relationship with issues of authority. Many feminist teachers know that teaching is an art form—narrative in much of its basic nature. The educator tells stories that link the past with the present and give continuity as the future is forged. These stories share the relationships, identities, powers, and authority of individuals in their community.

English-speaking women have experienced authority as it relates to their language. The Oxford English Dictionary relates *authority* to *author*—the one who makes something grow or originates something. That same dictionary then declares, "the author is the father who begets." Historical recall should refresh our awareness of how recently women authors wrote under male pseudonyms. Feminist theorists know that embodiment, sociality, and symbolization, among other things, are all gendered even when they appear to be neutral. The knowledge we have come to know through our experience does upset the order of what has been the father's narrative. We know there are those who refuse to recognize the women who struggle to speak a new gendered narration of the texts. *Her* art is illegitimate.

Traditionally women have been denied official participation

in the shaping of the themes of the community narrative. The story being told has reflected male concerns and interests. Women, unaware of this process, have been trapped into the faith of our fathers. So, there are ethical and intellectual questions about approaches to authority in our polycentric dilemmas of the global church and the teaching office.

Is The United Methodist Church ready to give a teaching office authority with recognition that the Latin *auctoritas* derives from the verb *augere*—to make or cause to grow, to originate? Such a perspective would emphasize the originating rather than restraining power of authority. This creating power becomes freedom, liberty, ability. Could feminist theological reflection exist in an *auctoritas* of *libertas* with *facultas*? Will freedom be encouraged, within which seekers who are committed to be faithful to the gospel may share their diversity of Christian experience? Will those on the margin share in the stream of teaching/learning? Or will there be an authority only on behalf of an elite who also judge what is authorized?

Feminists could enter into the freedom of discourse that would be the foundation toward the authorship that informs the work of the teaching office. That discourse, however, would require the emergence of a sense of community in which participants could trust that they might speak again of their encounter with the texts and traditions in their experience. Here the root meaning of *auctoritas* ("to grow") would strengthen the ethos to be responsible Christians. To know the meaning of discipleship is to invent it in our lives.

Some Reflections on Education

Feminist educational theory emerges from its examination of the structure and organization of our ideas regarding human knowledge and knowing processes. Feminist understanding is that interpretation begins in context. We experience the pervasiveness of gender as an ideological component through the patriarchal cultural order. Genderizations are socially constructed categories. The systems of patriarchal culture, including theological systems, need to be challenged to disclose the social/sexual assumptions that place value by birthright upon males. Dominance and submission, "insiders" and "outsiders," emerge from a patriarchal view that holds that the masculine will be the most valued perspective in life. Gender is not a neutral issue. Feminist educational discourse, therefore, seeks to disclose the overt and hidden contexts of oppression in patriarchal ideology.

Feminist educators hope, moreover, to reveal the possibilities of a new framework of valuing: a community of persons interconnected in a universe of connections striving to live in interdependent spiritual energy. Christian religious educators would thereby value all persons learning together.[2]

Women have not been authorized to be creators in patriarchal culture. Women have been charged to mind male creations both in the sense of obeying and tending. Thus woman may be teacher at home, at school, and at the domesticated church. Here she is to function as assistant to the legitimate processes of maintaining and recreating the authorized (patriarchal) culture.

These thoughts lead us to wonder whether the teaching office is a response to allow only a selected tradition to be worthy of knowing and of passing on to future generations. Is it an effort to create an official theology for the Wesleyan way? If so, feminists could not accept this form of minding the tradition.

We are also led to ask whether the form of the content (be it lectionary or other curriculum) is reductive in orientation. For example, is the canon used to create awareness of political and ethical differences so that hearers might sense both the debate of our time and intersecting antecedents at work in the relation of the church's teaching to daily life?

Behind various efforts to centralize curriculum, one finds an evolving alliance between the quest for "back to basics" among some conservative groups and the marketing issues of publishing houses. The curriculum may have more pictures of women—such as clergy persons or minority women in their traditional female roles—but one must still ask whether *their* texts, narratives, or experiences are being included in ways that their gender articulates a cogent reasoning to understand differences of meaning.

For feminists a positivist approach to Wesleyan knowledge would be considered inappropriate. The development of a Christian discipleship curriculum will need to be approached relationally. Attempts to develop understanding "to serve God and not mammon," for example, require meaningful interpretation among patterns of dominance and subordination. Our faith commitment is held amid the configurations of many interests. Since the church is part of the economic, political, and cultural spheres of interaction in which the dynamics of gender, race, and class participate, the production of what we teach is a part of these complications. To become clear about the function of the church in relation to society will require a relational education policy to guide the church's educational institutions, resources, and processes.

Lest the statement on behalf of feminism seem only mired in suspicion (even when born of experience), let me close with what I believe could be an affirmation of the role of a teaching office in the church.

1. In a time of cultural crisis, we need to ask: "What is politically and ethically justifiable knowledge for Christian discipleship and citizenship?" Attention to this issue would balance the quest for that which is authoritative with that which is also just.

2. In a time of reassessment of who and what we are called to be, the church needs to take account of the social nature of knowledge and the complications of oppression and liberation. The diversity of those who seek to be faithful (to their

commitment in Christian context in spite of patriarchy) needs to be heard toward the truth of the gospel. Those who will not confine the God of Jesus Christ to patriarchy believe they are dealing with questions the church should be facing anyway. Christian teaching/learning in our era must face issues of gender and human sexuality with candor within the household of faith and in discourse with the public.

3. Just as United Methodist women support a Committee on the Status and Role of Women (COSROW) in the life of the church, even though every agency in the church should be addressing the issues related to women, so also we could endorse within the institutional structures a teaching office. Every aspect of the church's life communicates and gives witness. A formal office related to teaching could focus on texts and contexts that need attention. Representative teaching offices in the conference system and in the Council of Bishops could focus specific questions of continuity, authority, and authenticity in the light of new circumstances and needed hermeneutics. Educators, aware of group and personal learning dynamics, can help with the structure of teaching/learning.

4. Christian feminists challenge the male systems that separate knowledge claims from the pragmatic and contextual nature of knowledge. We would share an overlapping vision, if "teaching" had the intention of helping The United Methodist Church to interpret Christian faith for a quality of life that develops within the community of faith and all of God's creation. Teaching biblical and/or theological studies for their own sake or the sake of "disembodied soul salvation" could be repudiated as primary objectives. There could be a legitimization of the dialogue of the people engaged in the practical necessity of living as disciples of Jesus Christ. Wrestling with choices of Christian stewardship, without the sense that there is a fixed end point, would help Christians to author their own

witness, strengthened by memory. The sense of mystery *with* the Holy One becomes a part of the open-ended hermeneutic conversation. Christian education could be freed from its encapsulated task of handing down a product. Congregational conversation could be freed to create communities where memory and vision are confirming and confronting. We could affirm the church as a place where the full being of each person could be present without pretensions. God's grace could be received. Education could become edifying.

A Closing Perspective

In acknowledging a crisis in the church fulfilling its teaching mission, concerned feminists might entreat responsible leadership to link teaching authority with learning empowerment. Teaching and learning have a new relationship with authority. The teacher is to enable learning not to control it. When teaching serves learning, authority is restored in the process.

Theological insights that will help persons understand faith embracing every aspect of their lives will involve critical reflection on the praxis of faith. To develop the profound relationship with meaningful symbols that give identity and empower action will require a contextual way of doing theological reflection, personally and communally. Internalized learning is rooted in our Methodist heritage.

Feminist spirituality could contribute to an evolving approach to the teaching office because it draws on the shaping of efficacious transformation. Our thought and praxis embody connectional collaboration, including God's present love and righteousness. Deliberation among our polycentric concerns could help God move us in new configurations of teaching to reveal new shapes of love and freedom.

NOTES

1. Audre Lord, *This Bridge Called My Back* (Watertown, Mass.: Persiphone Press, 1981), p. 99.
2. Scholarship of feminists is bringing educational materials to help in the construction of alternative interpretations. See, for example, S. B. Thistlethwaite and M. P. Engel, eds., *Lift Every Voice: Constructing Christian Theologies from the Underside* (San Francisco: Harper & Row, 1990).

Chapter 8

Recovery of the Teaching Office:
Insights from Education

Allen J. Moore

The teaching office is understood in this chapter as basically a religious office. The religious meaning of the office can be traced to the philosophical traditions of ancient Greece and Rome and to the rabbinical tradition of Judaism. Those religious meanings extended through the work of the founders of the early church. In our own era, however, teaching, like so many basic functions of society, has become separated from the religious and is centered in the secular community. The implications are clear: Teaching has lost its religious roots. It no longer has a sacred function in our secular society, and, with the possible exception of Judaism, it is no longer taken seriously by religious communities.[1]

The secularization of the office of teaching evolved over an extended time, largely due to the growing pluralism in North American society and to the inability of the churches to achieve a consensus on how to fulfill the educational needs of the nation, required by social change. The rise of the common school to serve both the public needs of society and the formative needs of the child was religiously motivated. The final collapse of the religious sources for the teaching function in public schools did not occur until well into this century. The churches have been reluctant ever since to struggle with the public meaning of teaching or the place of teaching within the religious community.

The religious character of teaching is still recognized in England and other Christian oriented societies in Europe. Schools and teachers are often located or identified with the parish church. Religious traditions are supported and observed as an integral part of the school's curriculum. Even in this country the educational experience itself is understood by some as having religious meaning, and the quest for quality in teaching has led some churches to assume again the mission of religious schooling.[2] Some persons have seriously proposed that mainline Protestant churches get back into general education in order to provide our society with alternative models of quality education and to enhance the validity of teaching within the religious community. This proposal would demonstrate what religious schools might look like in our time and how a truly liberal or humanistic concept of education could be achieved at the primary and secondary levels of schooling. Values and moral principles would not only be returned to education, but the transcending character of teaching might be recovered as well. Furthermore, a religiously motivated example of schooling could demonstrate how education could be effective with a pluralistic and multi-ethnic student body and faculty.[3]

The Recovery of Teaching

The concern for teaching and the recovery of the teaching office, however, is now primarily found in philosophical discussions on education. Those discussions occur in the context of a growing concern about the quality and character of contemporary education. Many believe teachers have

156

become primarily *managers* of classrooms and *technocrats* to the learning enterprise. Methods have dominated the curriculum, while content, setting, and the welfare of the community of learners have been neglected. The current debate in education centers on the failure of the common school to educate the whole of our student population. The drop-out rate continues to grow, especially among racial/ethnic students. Many persons graduate without the basic skills and understanding to function effectively in modern society. The response has been for most states to establish more formal standards and to quantify learning goals and objectives. The use of standardized tests of students' learning achievement has become a way in some school settings to measure the effectiveness of teachers. Church education has followed the trend. It has also sought to plan curriculum around the objectification of learning goals. In both public and church education less attention has been given to philosophical issues than to the technical side of education.

An emerging discussion of philosophical issues in education, especially at the post-secondary levels, has led to some educational changes. Harvard University School of Business has come to recognize that trained administrators must have help in sorting out the value options of a commercial society and in making moral decisions. The faculty plans to restore ethics to the curriculum because it has discovered that bright, rational, and technically competent young M.B.A.'s are ill equipped to make socially responsible decisions within the context of a global economy. The Claremont Graduate School has gone further in its graduate program in business with the assumption that the best graduate education in any profession, including business, is one grounded in the humanities. Its program involves more than exposure to the liberal arts. It engages students and other professional persons in lively discourse with the best thought in the humanities.

The role of the liberal arts in teacher education is also under discussion in university-based schools of education. Medicine and law have slowly come also to the recognition that technical competence alone does not make an effective doctor or lawyer. We have come to recognize that our society needs professionals who have a whole view of reality and who can do their work with wisdom. Professional and vocational educators in general have come to recognize that technical training and competence in one's field do not result in preparation to serve constructively in one's society. What is needed is the broad enrichment that comes from the liberal arts and the value orientation that comes from the study of the humanities. That point is made by Lawrence Cremin of Teachers College, who has written that a good education is a sustained and systematic effort to "acquire knowledge, attitudes, values, skills, [and] sensibilities."[4]

Two issues dominate the literature on general education today: the profession of the teacher and the subject-content of the common school. These issues are also relevant to the debate within religious education. In many ways, religious education would serve itself well if it would get outside its parochial preoccupation with the institutional decline of the churches and share in the public discourse on the role of the teacher and the place of education in the broader social reality. The recovery of the religious sensitivity (a progressive concept) of teaching and the religious nature of the office or profession of teacher would go far to improve the status of education in our public arena and the quality of teaching in our pluralistic society.

We are not talking about a sectarian view of religion or the teaching office. The particularity of the Christian vocation of the teacher is yet another agenda. Instead we are after the special religious or spiritual qualities that mark any good teacher. Whitehead has said a teacher truly engaged in education, be it history, mathematics, or religion, is involved in a religious task. He or she understands the "essence of education to be religious." This understanding leads to a new sense of duty and reverence for the whole of life.[5] In this regard, he caught what the ancient philosophers knew so well and what native and indigenous people still understand today about the teacher among the people. The excellent teacher is one who has a special quality—a sense of duty, worth, and reverence—that cannot readily be turned aside by secularization. The influence of the excellent teacher on the learner cannot be destroyed or denied. A good teacher is not only held in awe by students but also motivates them to new heights of achievement. These religious-like qualities enable persons to reach their "future possibility," or what Groome has called the "transcendent dimensions of life."[6]

The recovery of teaching as an honored profession with both intrinsic and extrinsic rewards is a growing need in general education. The role of the teacher in common education is influenced by political and economic factors. Donna H. Kerr of the Institute for Advanced Study at Princeton looks at the growing criticism leveled against teachers today. She notes not only the disenchantment of society with the teaching profession, but also the lack of satisfaction teachers experience from their work. She also notes that at least 50 percent of the teachers studied do not experience personal reward in their work. Kerr writes:

> A society's political and economic forces determine in what pursuits intellectual virtuosity will be rewarded. Neither with status nor with prestige nor with money do we reward teaching. We should not expect that we shall teach our young as competently as we could were our priorities otherwise.[7]

What seems to be true of the common school is also true of the church community at all levels. Teaching is both undervalued and underrewarded by the church. Those of us who are Christian educators are always trying to find a sense of worth in our vocation, and few directors of Christian education understand themselves primarily as teachers. Our work has come increasingly to be that of educational managers, or administrators of educational programs. We justify our existence by the apology that all that the church does is educate. Few of the powerful people in the local church understand their role as teachers. This includes the pastor, whose office includes a formal teaching function. Langford has already pointed out the fact that the teaching office lacks enough clarity and authority within The United Methodist Church to raise doubts about its existence (see chap. 3 of this book). Bishops, seminary professors, pastors, and Christian educators do not clearly see themselves in relation to the teaching role of the church. The exception is with the lay volunteer who has been recruited to do what the paid staff resists—that is, teach a Sunday school class.[8] We have often seen both passion and quality from those laypersons who understand that teaching is essential to the life of faith.

Possibly the situation within United Methodism has evolved because theology has such a minor role in the formation of the church's common life and has come to be associated largely with the academic life of the church. And yet, despite the fact that we are not a confessing denomination, our heritage also teaches us that all members share in doing theology. To profess faith carries with it the need to understand and to articulate that faith (to love God with both heart and mind).

The teaching office will have clarity and authority as the church is helped to discover the essential place teaching must occupy in the life of both the general church and the local congregation. That effort may begin with those of us who are called to education if we should claim our full vocation as teachers (doctors) of the church. We would then be following an example set by John Wesley, who remained a Fellow at Lincoln College, Oxford University, until his death. As a young priest of the Church of England, Wesley had been encouraged by his father to take up the duties of a parish minister. He resisted the invitation at the time, believing there was no Christian calling higher than that of a teacher. Even after he left Oxford to become an itinerant preacher in the Methodist movement, he continued to give much of his energies to educational ventures. It is almost incongruent with our beginnings as Methodist people to be in our current state of confusion over the priority of teaching for the salvation and growth of Christian people. Wesley's sense of a special responsibility for the common education of all people of eighteenth-century England should challenge our contemporary lack of attention to and participation in the reform of public education. In all likelihood, the recovery of teaching in the church will not come about until we begin to revalue the whole of education and participate in the discourse over the future of the education of all people.

Proposals for Educational Reform

Many proposals to reform education and the common school have been attempted. These have included new educational standards for teachers, with particular attention to general educational requirements and subject matter competence; state testing of competence for the credentialing of teachers; systems of accountability in which student achievement is tied to teacher evaluation; standardized tests of subject matter learning as a basis for school funding; and the use of a variety of objective evaluations for measuring classroom achievement. Although the results have been mixed, these efforts have generally been affirmed by the political system where the standards for education are now being set.

One of the most interesting developments has been the rise of fundamental schools and of magnet schools for gifted students. These schools tend to concentrate on basic studies and classical approaches to learning. In addition to the liberal arts and physical education, these schools also concentrate on grooming, good behavior and manners, citizenship, discipline, and high academic achievement. Basically, these schools are reproductions of the classical schools of the past and are grounded in the educational philosophy of essentialism.

New attention to essentialism has emerged in educational discourse largely due to the efforts of Mortimer Adler and the Paideia Group.[9] The schools organized around the essentialist concepts have apparently had some success in improving the learning achievement of students, and they have certainly provided a more enriched curriculum for the gifted person. In addition to a concern for the so-called three R's (reading, writing, and arithmetic), these schools have enjoyed expanded programs in literature, history, the arts, and, in some cases, religion and philosophy. It must be noted, however, that a host of children are eliminated from these schools because of a lack of readiness or relevance to the social needs of many young people. The *Paideia Proposal* and the schools that reflect its philosophy go against a long current of democratic reform in education to give all persons the kind of education they most need and to make educational resources available to all students. The common school, since the progressive era of reform, has become the symbol of equality in American society and has sought to ensure that a quality education will be available to every individual regardless of economic and social circumstance.[10]

The discussions of the *Paideia Proposal* have focused

attention on what we mean by quality education and emphasized the special needs of some students who are gifted. The proposal has encouraged a journey of depth into learning and the importance of leadership development. The *Paideia Proposal* seeks teachers, not from schools or departments of education, but from liberal arts universities. Good teachers are identified as those who are knowledgeable, who have learned to be good thinkers, and who have organized for themselves a view of life that is worth sharing. This religious view of the teacher may be the most important contribution coming from the neo-essentialist movement. Although the didactic role of teaching is important, the teacher is understood also as a tutor or a coach who places attention on the intellectual dialogue with students. The goal is to stimulate the intellectual development of the learner through dialogue around the ideas, values, and beliefs of great thinkers.

Another of the important and far-reaching proposals for the improvement of teaching comes from the work of Donald A. Schön, Ford Professor of Urban Studies and Education at the Massachusetts Institute of Technology.[11] Schön has collaborated with Chris Argyris in a significant study of learning that takes place within the context of one's work.[12] His most recent work on the role of the teacher in professional education has already had significant impact on theological education and may have important implications for the training of church educators.[13] The importance of Schön's book is his proposal that we rethink what it means to be a teacher and how good teachers are formed. He shares Whitehead's idea that teaching is an artistic act.[14]

Schön believes a new understanding of professional education, including teacher education, requires a new "epistemology of practice" and a new set of philosophical questions. He is critical of the "technical rationality" that has preoccupied education today. Not only has the positivist view of teaching reduced the place of values and meaning (world view and philosophy for life), but also it has resulted in making education, especially professional education, largely performance learning, task accomplishment, and the learning of functional skills. A person educated in this way can usually solve the immediate problem at hand, but often lacks understanding of the larger problems of society or a whole view of human existence. Specialization results in dividing reality into segments that for many persons never get put together.

While Adler, on one hand, is critical of what he sees as the excesses of progressivism, Schön sees value in the recovery of that philosophical tradition and calls for a new reading of Dewey and others in an effort to eliminate the sharp distinction in educational circles between theory and practice, the classical and the practical, and the systematic and the applied. His interest is in the unity of knowledge and the larger questions of human life. He is concerned not just with the ability to build a good road, but also with the ability to deal with why the road should be built and what the long-term consequences of a new road may be.

Schön suggests that a teacher should be a co-participant in the learning process—what he calls "education for artistry." For Schön, "artistry" is a kind of intuitive knowledge that cannot be readily articulated or rationalized even though its truth is apparent. It is not just the knowledge we gain after practice, but that which comes, sometimes suddenly, in the midst of the practice—what he calls "knowing-in-practice." Artistry seems abstract at first, but it refers to those special qualities of professional performance that set some persons apart from the routine performer. Words like *wisdom, talent,* and *intuition* all catch up the artistry Schön is striving for in teaching and in professional education. "Artistry is an exercise of intelligence, a kind of knowing . . . rigorous in its own terms.''[15] It is the art of problem framing, of implementation, and of improvisation. Education in artistry is the development through practice until those sensibilities of judgment, insight, and actions are formed into what Schön calls ''knowing that'' or ''thinking what I am doing'' rather than always ''thinking WHAT to do and doing it.''[16] The classroom in this situation becomes more like a design center or an artist's studio. Learning to be a good teacher requires a classroom and a coach who works with the student teacher to develop intuitive leadership with the learners. Judgments regarding learning are made during the ordinary interchange; qualitative experiences are the aim. Teaching is an aesthetic quality that marks the difference between simply performing and creating an artistic expression.

Schön's contribution is not only his vision of professional education in general, but in the way he calls into question the assumptions that are implicit in both teacher education and theological education. More important, he would agree with the proposals coming from Adler and others. He would send us back to Dewey, Whitehead, and other philosophers of liberal education. The real issue in contemporary education, however, is not with any particular philosophical system, but with the problem that the current philosophy of education is, in fact, no philosophy.

Bloom and Hirsch

The extent to which philosophy may open the road ahead to an invigorated discussion of education and the role of the teacher is evident in the attention given to two recent books. The first is an apology for an essentialist education by Allan Bloom.[17] Bloom wants people to identify fully with the cultural traditions of the West and to appreciate and appropriate that tradition as fully as possible. He criticizes our contemporary culture, believing that it lacks standards or norms. He believes pluralism leads to cultural relativism. He considers "the loss of reason," or the neglect of culture, to be one of the negative consequences of modernity. What he means by reason is to be informed by the great thinkers of the Western culture.

Bloom's work fails to address adequately the multicultural context of our time and the validity of the non-Western experience. His proposal actually runs the risk of "closing the American mind" to the rich traditions of the East, as well as to the growing influence of native cultures.

The values of the Bloom proposal are basically two. Education should result in persons' standing for something significant, and knowledge needs to be precise and integrative. As any of us would readily agree, these seem on the surface to be worthy goals. They do not make clear what norms or standards for truth and which basic studies will serve the future of a world society in which increased understanding and appreciation of the many people of our society are required. Increasingly, the fate of any one of us is tied to the fate of everyone else. Bloom's view of social reality must be critically assessed if we are to take seriously any new revival of an essentialist view of education.

For many educators, *Cultural Literacy: What Every American Needs to Know,* by E. D. Hirsch, Jr., is a far more helpful work. He also raises the question as to which *content* is most appropriate to be mastered by a well-educated person today (what Hirsch calls "cultural literacy"). He describes this body of content both in broad generalization as well as in an extended list of specifics. "To be culturally literate," for Hirsch, "is to possess the basic information needed to thrive in the modern world."[18] He is concerned with how culture is achieved, and, for him, this requires inculcating in students a rather extensive list of ideas, concepts, and symbolic phrases. The proposal seeks also to improve the quality of schooling and to help persons achieve a high level of excellence in learning. He rejects the prescriptive approach to content that is characteristic of essentialism. Instead, he gives attention to describing how the goal of literacy would form the curriculum of the school.

Hirsch critiques the "content-neutral" character of current curriculum. He argues that life-experience curriculum, or education as personal enrichment, does not adequately prepare persons to participate effectively in community. For him, a community is both enriched and made more productive when persons share common information and a core of ideas so they can engage in a learned discourse. Even though Hirsch would not discourage "natural learning" (see also Rousseau), his concern is with a "specific" curriculum (see also Plato).[19] In this regard, Hirsch is more a traditionalist than a reformist in education.

"Cultural literacy" may be understood from an anthropological perspective. Persons are inculcated into their culture as they come to share similar values, beliefs, and symbol-systems. Especially important is the language and the vocabulary they learn to use in communication. An important assumption behind Hirsch's study is that a specific literacy is required to form a people and to ensure the future of a society. He writes regarding this concern: "Only by accumulating shared symbols, and the shared information that the symbols represent, can we learn to communicate effectively with one another in our national community."[20] All of this seems good, but the nationalism here represented would be an issue for many liberal educators who would argue that the urgent need at this time is the forming of an international culture in which persons from a variety of societies learn how to share common concerns, communicate about important matters, and forge a new kind of global society.

Implications for the Teaching Office

This survey of some important developments in education is admittedly superficial. Others might choose different issues of concern,[21] but I believe it may suggest several useful insights for our discussion of the church's teaching office. We turn now to some learnings and implications.

1. If Thomas Langford is correct, and I believe he is, the teaching office, and its authority, in The United Methodist Church is either non-existent, or at best, unclear and diffused. This is true at all levels, including the episcopacy, the theological professor, the pastor, and the educational minister. A basic assumption in this chapter is that the teaching office of the church will finally find clarity as the church enters seriously into the public discourse regarding teaching in general, including discourse about the role of the teacher in the common school. This assumption is based on another. All forms of education in modern society are interdependent. If we do not look beyond our parochial needs, the concept of teacher will consequently escape us.

Careful and scholarly work is needed to recover and define for United Methodism the meaning and authority of teaching within our tradition. We have within our historical experience the sources for a revitalized office of teaching, especially within the local congregation. Teaching historically was central to the ministry of the local church. Today, in Third World churches and other indigenous churches, teaching in the local church has become inseparable to the ongoing theological enterprise of the larger church. In Europe, Africa, and Asia the sharp distinction between the theological school and the church is not made. Pastors often understand themselves as being scholars of the church, and they see scholarly work and theological teaching as normal in their calling to ministry. The "theology by the people" movement of the World Council of Churches has actually called for theological teaching to be shifted from the school to the church.[22]

As we have already seen, John Wesley himself was a teacher, and many considered him to be the most important leader in education in eighteenth-century England. His leadership led to the reform of education in England, and he contributed largely to the rise of the English common school. Wesley believed that education was essential to the religious life ("Let us unite the two so long divided—knowledge and vital piety"). For him, the good news of the gospel ("grace of God's love") meant that people had a new capacity to change, to learn, to read, to improve their minds, and to grow in the knowledge of God's love for the world. The universal love already given by God and experienced in salvation was an ongoing event in the lives of persons (sanctification). Outler points out that the reason Methodists placed so much emphasis on education was their belief that people needed to grow in the awareness of grace and what it means to live a life under the grace of God (knowledge of going on to an ever more perfect life in God). Teaching was not an exceptional office for the early Methodists, but was a compelling task that could not be avoided. The growth of Sunday schools, class meetings, and schools and colleges in England and America marked the urgency of teaching for the movement.

2. The office of the Christian educator needs to be reevaluated by both the church and the profession. The director of Christian education emerged within a particular historical context (the rise of the large institutional or programmatic church and the development of the religious education movement). The professional role of the church educator has not translated well into other cultural or church contexts (e.g., the black or ethnic church or indigenous national churches). The director of Christian education was formed within the rise of liberalism and progressivism in the

theological and philosophical. In the many discussions regarding Christian education, we have been hard pushed to explain how it can be relevant to other than majority church and cultural settings, why explicit programs of Christian education have declined at all levels of the church, and what roles are needed for the future.

I, for one, believe that these are worthy issues to study. Along with these concerns, we need to discuss a metaphor of "teacher" that would engage both ecumenical and public school thought. We also need to explore models of education in Third World churches.[23] If we are to renew the office of teacher, we will need to face political questions as to who serves in the office and how the office will affect the work of pastor, associate pastor, and director of Christian education. What especially will be the implications for the aging institution of Sunday school and the relationships of congregations to theological schools? An example of a model worth exploring within the ecumenical discourse is the understanding within the Russian Orthodox Church that religious education is a function of theological education. This means that curriculum development and teacher training, for example, are tasks shared with the theological school.[24]

3. The issue of content in the teaching life of the church remains critical. What is to be taught dominates the delivery system of the curriculum and includes what people want and what will sell. Content seems to be largely determined by marketing rather than by the authority of the church. In another sense, this is the nature of Methodism. Our theology is pragmatic and grows out of both perceived needs and the practical concerns of the church. Often the nature of our theological discourse is dominated by practical and political concerns: What is the content that speaks to our needs today? What will help us grow and compete with the more evangelical churches? The pragmatic nature of our church's

life leads us sooner or later to the struggle with Scripture as the essential content for our teaching. The conclusion that the Bible is the essential content biases us toward the essentialist view of education, although the spirit of the Christian education profession has been in the direction of neo-progressivism. Essentialists, on the other hand, would broaden the curriculum to include, at least, history, Christian thought, art, Christian literature, and other branches of theology.

The current debate over the place of Scripture in the life of the church and in the content (curriculum resources) for teaching should not cloud the fact that The United Methodist Church is not a biblical church in the same sense that some other denominations are. The living core of our self-understanding as a Christian group is larger than Scripture. We seek to balance the importance of Scripture with attention to tradition, experience, and reason. We are also a doctrinal church with strong Anglican and Roman Catholic roots. We have preserved the Articles of Religion as historical statements and maintained a strong sacramental life. At the same time, we are a confessing church in the Reformed tradition with our links to the Confession of Faith of the former Evangelical United Brethren Church.

We do understand Scripture as the story of our salvation through the life of the Hebrew people and the events of Jesus Christ. This is a story that we all need to know and understand. But nowhere, not even in the official theological statement of 1988, do we believe that the essential content of our faith is limited to the Bible. The study of Scripture is not an end in itself, but a means to our theological self-understanding. Our theological task is much more complex and encompassing as we seek to understand and articulate our faith for the church and for the world. John Wesley would ask as part of the agenda of the early Conferences, ''What to teach?'' And the answer remains today, ''The substance of the gospel.'' The office of teacher requires us to clarify our theological task for the church and the world and to come to increased clarity as to what the essential content is for the church. The issue of specific content is as worthy for church discussion as it is for public debate. Personal growth and enrichment are important dimensions of education, but the issue remains as what is required to make United Methodists "culturally literate" with a common language or symbol system and a shared vision of our life together.[25]

Farley and others have written that it has been almost an accident of history that theological study was removed from the life of the congregation and placed primarily in the schools of the church.[26] The questions that have emerged in ecumenical discourse are over who owns theology and who does theology. The answer is that the church and all of the people of the church engage in theological study and discourse. I would propose here that theological study is the essential task of the local congregation. Farley writes that "church education should be theological education in the full and rigorous sense of ordered learning."[27] All believers, and not just the clergy, have the need to engage in the study that will lead to what Farley calls "reflective wisdom" (defined as "the interpretation of tradition, action, truth, and work as they come together in situations").[28] Hough and Cobb, in writing about Farley's theologia, say: "Theologia is reflective understanding, shared by members of a Christian community regarding who they are and what they are to do, given their concrete world-historical situation."[29] Such an essentialist view of Christian teaching within a local congregation could help believers to develop informed convictions that will not only serve the needs of the church but will also enable them through study and action to address the urgent issues of our world situation.

4. Finally, a continued study of public or common education could lead us again into a discourse about the philosophical bases for education in the church and in the common school. General education is asking philosophical questions—the kinds of questions that at the turn of the century called modern religious education into being. The dialogue between theology and philosophy and between church and school provided at that time a rich environment for educational reform and for informed political action. The recovery of the office of teaching will not come from within the church alone but from the reform of society as the teacher gains public authority and respect once again.

NOTES

1. See Robert Ulich, *The History of Religious Education* (New York: New York University Press, 1968).

2. Parochial education in this country sometimes serves as a credible alternative to the common school but often serves to foster elitism and racial segregation.

3. The source of this proposal is from F. Thomas Trotter, formerly General Secretary, Board of Higher Education and Ministry, and now President, Alaska Pacific University, Anchorage, Alaska.

4. Lawrence A. Cremin, *Traditions of American Education* (New York: Basic Books, 1977), p. 134.

5. See Alfred North Whitehead, *The Aims of Education* (New York: Free Press, 1967), p. 14.

6. Thomas H. Groome, *Christian Religious Education* (San Francisco: Harper & Row, 1980), p. 22.

7. Donna H. Kerr, "Teaching Competence and Teacher Education in the United States," *Teacher College Record* 84, 3 (1983): 531.

8. The relation of the teaching office to the lay Sunday school worker deserves more attention than it has received. In fact, some would argue that the professionalization of education and the formalization of teaching have led to the current confusion as to who are the "teachers" of the church.

9. See Mortimer Adler, *The Paideia Proposal* (New York: Macmillan, 1982), and Adler, ed., *Paideia Problems and Possibilities* (New York: Macmillan, 1983). Adler and his followers tend to ignore the underprivileged in public education, the underclass, the ethnic minority, the learning handicapped, and the marginal learner. All of these are in need of educational achievement to function in our society. Studies point to the possibility of all these groups becoming educationally effective when the system has them as a major goal.

10. A good review of the pros and cons of the Paideia proposals can be found in "The Paideia Proposal: A Symposium," *Harvard Educational Review* 53, 4 (1983): 377-411.

11. See Donald A. Schön, *Educating the Reflective Practitioner* (San Francisco: Jossey-Bass Publishers, 1987).

12. See, for example, C. Argyris and D. Schön, *Theory in Practice: Increasing Professional Effectiveness* (San Francisco: Jossey-Bass, 1974); and *Organizational Learning* (Reading, Mass.: Addison-Wesley, 1978).

13. See especially Joseph C. Hough, Jr., and John B. Cobb, Jr., *Christian Identity and Theological Education* (Chico, Calif.: Scholars Press, 1985). Hough and Cobb believe it is important to clarify the changing leadership needs of the church. They seem to believe, along with others today, such as Don Browning and Edward Farley, that church leadership may best be understood within the context of practical theology. The domination of clergy paradigm in theological education is seriously under review by these scholars.

14. Whitehead writes, "Education is the guidance of the individual towards a comprehension of the art of life: and by the art of life I mean the most complete achievement of varied activity expressing the potentialities of that living creature in the face of its actual environment. . . . The art of life is the guidance of this adventure." *The Aims of Education,* p. 39.

15. *Educating the Reflective Practitioner,* p. 13; see also pp. 1-44.

16. Ibid., p. 22. Schön draws upon Gilbert Ryle in the quote and is cited on p. 22.

17. Allan Bloom, *The Closing of the American Mind: How Higher Education Has Failed Democracy and Impoverished the Souls of Today's Students* (New York: Simon and Schuster, 1987).

18. E. D. Hirsch, Jr., *Cultural Literacy: What Every American Needs to Know* (Boston: Houghton Mifflin Co. 1987), p. xiii.

19. Hirsch agrees with Plato that the goal of education is "to choose and promote our best traditions." Ibid., p. xvi.

20. Ibid., p. xviii.

21. The writings of the reconceptualists were not included here because of space and because they have been discussed by others already. Among the many contributions they make is the recognition that all education is political in nature. The teaching office is, among other things, a political issue in United Methodism. This includes status of the office, the priority education holds in the church, and the current struggle to control theological content and process. For example, see William Pinar, *Curriculum Theorizing: The Reconceptualists* (Berkeley, Calif.: McCutchan Pub., 1974).

22. See John S. Pobee, ed., *Theology By the People: Reflections on Doing Theology in Community* (Geneva: Theological Education Section of the World Council of Churches, 1986).

23. The literature of the World Council of Churches is very rich in this regard. See the catalog of publications as well as the variety of study documents from the several sections of the WCC. For information write U.S. Office of the WCC, 475 Riverside Drive, Room 915, New York, NY 10115-0050.

24. See *Religious Education in the Russian Orthodox Church* (New York and Geneva: World Council of Churches, 1978).

25. A much more definitive discussion of this issue of theology can be found in chapter 5 of this book, "Our Teaching Task: Scripture in a Wesleyan Context," by Mary Elizabeth Mullins Moore.

26. See especially Edward Farley, *Theologia: The Fragmentation and Unity of Theological Education* (Philadelphia: Fortress Press, 1983).

27. Edward Farley, *The Fragility of Knowledge* (Philadelphia: Fortress Press, 1988), p. 175.

28. Ibid., p. 173.

29. Hough and Cobb, *Christian Identity and Theological Education*, p. 3.